"We're Up by Over 150 Children in Our 5 Locations Since Working with Kris"

"Working with Kris has been the single most important thing we've done to grow our enrollment. Quite simply we would not be where we are today without her expertise. As a husband-wife team of 5 large locations, we've gotten a huge return on investment from working with her. Save yourself lots of time, money and frustration and use Kris as a coach and mentor – I promise you will not regret it."

~Gerry Pastor with wife Jane Porterfield, Owners
Educational Playcare
5 locations near Hartford, CT

"Kris Murray's Ideas Resulted in Over $540,000 in Future Tuition Revenue!"

"When I attended Kris Murray's conference,I took home 72 actionable ideas to grow my child care centers. I only implemented TWO of those ideas and that resulted in 38 new children enrolled in just over 3 months. That will bring our business over $540,000 in future revenue. That ain't monopoly money, Kris…that's "we're goin' to Hawaii for our 35th Wedding Anniversary money!" While my wife, Cindy, didn't make it to the conference can you guess that she's a fan :-)!? Thanks for all your help!"

~Bob Kuehner, Owner
Amazing Kids
Pelham, AL

"You WILL save time & an un-measurable amount of money!"

"Kris is the ONLY child care marketing expert and professional I've been able to find that is worth investing in. She has oodles of experience and knowledge that helped get me up and on my feet within weeks! Kris takes the time, knows her clients by name, and is personally invested in each and every one of her students. You WILL save time & an un-measurable amount of money in your child care business with all the knowledge, tips, and expert know-how in Kris's programs. I know because I have now been an Insiders Circle member for almost FOUR years!"

Trent, Kelley, Casey, Norah

~Kelley Ebert, Owner
Family Traditions Child Care
Bexley, OH

"100 New Enrollments in Two Months Since Joining Kris Murray's Mastermind Group!"

"Over the past 2 months our 5 preschools started over 100 new students while obtaining deposits from another 60 students for next fall. Our company was stagnant for many years; Kris Murray provided helpful tools to create positive marketing momentum and leadership development in a short time span. I credit much of our new found enrollment success to the marketing techniques and tips provided by Kris Murray and her website."

~Scott Lieberman, Co-Owner
  Woodcrest Schools
  Tarzana, CA

"Increased WEEKLY revenue by over $5,000/week."

"Our weekly tuition was down to a scary low weekly income in January. (We have a large center with a large payroll and budget) Normally it rebounds quickly after the holidays, but this year it was not coming back up as fast as we would have liked to have seen. I am happy to say that at this point we have increased our WEEKLY revenue by over $5,000.00 per week. I have to attribute much of that growth to implementing all of the ideas Kris has given us."

~Donna Jensen, Owner
  The Learning Station
  Conway, SC

"We Are Finally Enrolling New Children! Tripled Enrollment in 1 Location"

"**Superb Training!** In my 25 plus years in the business, I have only once had training of this caliber! Kris has taken marketing to the next level! I feel rejuvenated! **We tripled our enrollment in one of our locations (from 30 to 90 children) in just a few months using the Enrollment Boot Camp techniques.** I no longer feel like my marketing efforts are fruitless and a waste of money. All of my center management are more motivated than ever. We are Facebooking and emailing and videoing and most importantly of all **ENROLLING new children!**"

~Annette Gentry
  Exec. Director, Creative Day School
  Greensboro, NC

"The missing link for anyone providing child care."

"Kris is the missing link for anyone providing child care. Whether you are a multiple center owner, a small center owner, or family provider she has the answers. **When you have Kris' input you have the information of being a franchise without franchise fees.** She, along with her husband Devin, are an incredible team. You are still in business for yourself but no longer by yourself. She is an awesome mentor."

~Don Sutton, Owner
 Crowned Hart Preschools
 St Augustine, FL

"A wealth of invaluable information."

"Kris and Devin Murray are an excellent resource for marketing information specific to the child care industry. If you're fairly experienced in marketing, as I am, you will still greatly benefit from their information. They have a fresh take on some areas and, of course, holding yourself accountable by staying connected with marketing messages keeps us on track. If you are new to marketing, then you

will have a wealth of invaluable information to start with...ideas that are very usable."

~Paula Bonesteel, Owner
 Sunshine House
 Concord, CA

"I Opened My Brand New Center FULLY Enrolled With a Waiting List of 48!"

"Kris – Your program has been incredibly invaluable to me! My biggest concern was whether I would have enough kids when I opened the doors to make the venture profitable. I followed your system and guess what...when I opened doors on Jan 4th, 2010, I was AT FULL CAPACITY with a waiting list of 48 children. The

parents are loving it & telling their friends & neighbors to get on the wait list. Kris, this program will work for everyone if they apply each & every principle exactly as you outline it, no guesswork & no surprises. Thank you for giving me the tools I need to make my dream of a successful business venture come true!"

~Ms. Carmen Stine, Owner
 Bronx, New York

"In just 3 short months, I increased my enrollment 49%!"

"I found Kris Murray and absolutely love what her program has done for my business! She has taught me to look at my business in a whole different light. I have learned so many tools to help grow my business! In just 3 short months, I **increased my enrollment 49%! AMAZING!"**

~Aleta Mechtel, Owner
Children of Tomorrow
Chanhassen, MN

"Kris Murray Knows What Works – We Are Proof of That!"

"Kris helped us turn our center's enrollment around completely. When she started working with us, we were really hurting for enrollments. It's been 11 months, and we are now VERY close to capacity, and actually taking a waiting list for our Kindergarten program! Kris Murray truly cares about early childhood and has a passion for helping others. Not only that, she knows what works – we are living proof of that! We cannot thank you enough, Kris!"

~Alison Pfeister, Owner
TLC Child Development Center
Hudson, OH

"We Are at Record Enrollment!"

"Since joining Kris Murray's Gold Core Coaching ProgramI have completed my operations manual and 2014 marketing calendar. My January numbers we are at 96% FTE (that's a record) and we also have small wait lists started in some classrooms. I have more clarity on how to accomplish my personal and professional goals and I am thrilled to see what this year brings. Thanks Kris for all you do for us!"

~Kristen Fisher, Director
Foundations Early Childhood Education Center
Port Charlotte, FL

The 77 Best Strategies to Grow Your Early Childhood Program

Proven, Cutting-Edge Ideas Your Competitors Are Probably Not Using

KRIS MURRAY

Published by Child Care Marketing Solutions
PO Box 3107
Crested Butte, CO 81224
www.childcare-marketing.com

First edition 2014
Printed in the United States of America

Acknowledgements

Many people helped support me and keep things humming along at our company while my attention was focused on this book. I'd like to thank my team at Child Care Marketing Solutions: Camille St. Martin for helping me get the book formatted and being an overall excellent team member; Jillian Rosich for helping take care of our valued clients and members; and most of all my wonderful and talented husband and partner Devin Murray. I could not have created this book without your support and encouragement.

Thanks to Vernon Mason for providing a wonderful Foreword for this book. You are an inspiration to many in our field.

Thank you to my book designer Rosamond Grupp for your timely help and talented work.

Finally, a huge thank you to all my clients who took the time to contribute a Case Study for this book. Your success stories are an inspiration to others, and demonstrate that the ideas in this book not only work but are being put into practice by successful early childhood professionals all over the world.

This book is dedicated to my children,
Owen and Maeve.

Contents

Foreword

When Kris asked me to write the foreword for this book, I was so honored and excited. I believe that Kris Murray is the best thing to happen to the childcare industry in decades. She never ceases to amaze me with her understanding of our industry. She develops exactly what we need and sometimes things we don't even know we need. She's provided us with a book that is an easy to use bounty of resources with a step by step guide on how to improve your childcare business. Buying and using this book is the first step to a better tomorrow for you and the families in your care. Kris teaches from the heart, never losing sight of the importance of the quality of the care we provide. With her contagious enthusiasm, you can't help but be inspired.

I sent Kris an email a few months ago that said, "Your influence on this field that many folks looked at as stagnant is astounding! I wonder how many folks you pulled out of burnout, how many programs you've saved and people you've help push to the next level???? Just wanted to say you're amazing!" I sent this after one of her inspiring conference calls. When I met Kris the timing was perfect, I had just transitioned from a single site to four locations. She inspired me to kick it into high gear….get out of my own way, stop settling for survival and push for thriving…..success beyond what I had envisioned.

I've implemented her strategies and my enrollment improved, my website is better, I have awesome parent testimonials and my Directors are better trained on handling phone inquiries, tours, and the all-important asking for the enrollment.

Kris understands that our industry is synonymous with low profit, few resources and scarce time. She has invested her time developing strategies that are spot on, concise, and tested. She has the best information and most times, the only information that is tailored specifically for the childcare industry. Kris' techniques will challenge you to do more and to be more. Her books are becoming must reads, if not the Bible for improving the business side of your childcare program. She believes that she succeeds only when we are successful. Her new book gives our industry the tools to thrive! No matter the level your business is currently, there is something for everyone whether you are an Owner, Director or both. So if you are looking for the next step to improve your childcare program, this book is for you!

> — *Vernon H. Mason, Jr. is President of WEE SCHOOL Child Development Centers in North Carolina. He is known as a Humorist, inspiring Keynote Speaker and Workshop Trainer Extraordinaire.*

Introduction

Do you need some fresh ideas for growing your enrollment? Are you frustrated that you spend many hours on your marketing and advertising, with little results to show for it? Or maybe you aren't spending much time or budget on marketing at all, because you have no earthly idea where to begin. Either way, this book is for you.

I have worked exclusively with owners and directors of early childhood programs since 2009, and I have spent hundreds if not thousands of hours inside child care programs around North America. I know what it's like to walk in your shoes. If you're like most of my clients, here are some of your biggest challenges, frustrations, and complaints:

- You work long hours on a seemingly endless list of administrative and managerial tasks.
- You aren't able to work "on" your business enough because you are too busy working in the day to day operations and fighting fires.
- You aren't spending enough time marketing your business, so your enrollment is lower than you'd like it to be.
- You don't have systems in your marketing – you randomly and haphazardly try ideas as they come into your mind.
- You are not tracking your marketing metrics so you don't have a clue what's working or how you are doing at converting prospects to enrollments.
- You struggle with keeping quality staff, so you spend a lot of time hiring and training – and you may even be forced to spend time in the classroom, cook meals, etc.

The first step to turning your business around is to maximize your revenue and cash flow, so you can address some of these operational issues. When you are fully enrolled, you can delegate more (to people you can afford to hire), pay teachers a higher wage, invest more in your infrastructure and quality, and of course, spend more on marketing so you STAY full.

Therefore, the goal of this book is to hand you easy-to-implement ideas that can help you get fully enrolled with a waiting list. And not just any old ideas – these are the 77 BEST ideas and strategies we use consistently. I have helped hundreds of owners grow their enrollment by 15 to 300 percent in just a few months, so I know it's possible for you. In fact, we've included some of their case studies and results from using the ideas in this book, to provide you with proof and inspiration.

> **RESOURCE**
> If you don't yet have my first book, **The Ultimate Child Care Marketing Guide**, you may want to head over to Amazon or RedleafPress.org to get a copy. It's a great accompanying resource to the book you are holding right now.

My first book, "The Ultimate Child Care Marketing Guide", has sold thousands of copies and is 5-star rated on Amazon. I wrote this, my second book, as an easy-to-use idea generator. Anytime you need a boost in creativity for building enrollment, you can consult this book as your idea resource. Pick one or two ideas that appeal to you, and get started.

How to Use this Book

The 77 strategies and ideas presented in this book are categorized into 8 important topic areas. You can read the book from cover to cover, identifying strategies that you'd like to test and try. Or, you can hone in on a specific topic area that's of top importance and priority to you. Either way, you'll come away with fresh ideas for growing your child care center or preschool.

There are 12 case studies included in this book, each directly tied to a specific idea presented in the book. You'll find each case study on the page directly following the related idea.

Where appropriate and useful, *Resource* boxes are provided on the right-hand side of the page, like the one shown above. These are designed to give you extra help and tools for specific ideas, to help you take your knowledge and skill set beyond what's provided in this book.

Lead Generation Ideas: How to Grow Your Inquiries

IDEA #1
Build Your "House List"

What is a house list and why is it useful? A house list is another name for a customer / prospect DATABASE. It's a list you build in-house that includes segments of important people regarding the health of your business. Ideally, those segments would include current customers, prospects, past customers or graduated families, and perhaps a list of community partners including business referral partners.

When you have a house list, you have a powerful asset for your child care business. You have the ability to

> **RESOURCES**
> - ChildCare CRM is the only list-building software built from the ground up for our industry. Learn more and get a free demo at: **www.childcarecrm.com/krismurray**
> - There's a lot that goes into successful list-building that we don't have time to cover here. Get more in-depth step by step training at: **www.childcare-marketing.com/list-building**

reach out to your list and communicate with them whenever you like. Ideally, you have email addresses, physical mailing addresses, and phone numbers for all the contacts on your list, so you can reach out to them via multiple methods of media. You could also collect birthdays, children's names, employer name, and other valuable data in this list.

Let's say you start building your list, using a customer relationship management (CRM) software such as ChildCare CRM. You set up your segmented groups and are able to grow your list to over 1,000 families in just over a year (by the way, this is a realistic goal for small businesses like child care centers). Now you are able to send your monthly e-newsletter to your list, as well as weekly articles and videos featuring parenting tips and fun events happening in your center. Can you see the power of your "list"? Whenever you have an opening in your program, you could send a message to a sub-set of your list, letting them know. Or tell them you just added a new Baby Yoga class.

If you don't have a house list, you are leaving enrollments – and revenue – on the table.

IDEA #2
Be Found on the Map

This idea is all about being found ONLINE, of course. Google, Yahoo, Bing, and the other search engines all serve local brick and mortar businesses by providing searchers with the map locations of the service or product they're looking for. However, if you have not claimed your local listing (in other words, let the search engines know where you're located and that you are a real and legitimate business providing child care services) then you risk being left OFF the local map entirely.

This is a huge mistake that we see many early childhood businesses

> **RESOURCE**
> My husband Devin Murray literally "wrote the book" on online marketing for the child care industry, including simple tips to get your program on the map. The book is called *Child Care Marketing Online* and it's available at Amazon.com both in hard-copy and Kindle versions.

making. Because you don't know how to claim your listing, along with other techniques to get ranked higher in the search engine results (such as *Idea #8: Getting Online Reviews*, on page 9), you may not be showing up on the map for your keywords.

What are keywords? They are the top phrases or words prospective parents are using to search for child care. Primary keywords for our industry typically include "daycare", "preschool", "child care", and "after school programs". Secondary keywords include things like "infant care", "pre-K", and "best daycare". You want to show up in your market on the map for all these keywords, and there's some art as well as science to getting it right.

It's worth the effort, however. I've known early childhood programs who almost instantly TRIPLE the number of inquiries they get, just by getting near the top of the local map results.

IDEA #3

Use Pay-per-Click Advertising

RESOURCES

- I have learned most of what I know about Google Adwords from one of the masters, Perry Marshall. His book, The Ultimate Guide to Google Adwords, is the bible of this topic. You can find it on Amazon.

- For a step-by-step training guide on Adwords for Child Care, check out our Adwords Academy training course here: **www. childcare-marketing.com/adwords-academy**

Also known as Google Adwords, pay-per-click advertising is probably the fastest way to reach hundreds or even thousands of online prospects in your local market. To see current examples of pay-per-click ads in your market, open a browser window and type in "child care" in the search field.

You'll see the results - current ads that are running - on the right-hand side of the page, and perhaps one or two at the top of the page. Make a note of which of your competitors are advertising, and what their ads say. Which ones have the best copy? Which ones stand out from the crowd? Using Adwords is a great way to get online prospects to visit your website and learn more about you, and you can show up for any keyword you choose, as long as you put it in your Adwords campaign. You can set a daily budget limit and select the geographic location, days, and hours your campaign will run. You can also select the maximum amount you "bid" per click, and Google gives you a good idea of how much to bid in order to get your ad seen.

Google Adwords gives you many opportunities and advantages in your marketing. These include speed, testing, reach, and the ability to track your return-on-investment (ROI).

- *Speed*: Compared to traditional forms of advertising, Adwords is fast. Really fast. You can have a campaign up and running from scratch in under 10 minutes.

- *Testing*: You can use Adwords to test headlines, offers, and program ideas. It's like a mini online focus group.

- *Reach:* you can run highly targeted campaigns, and reach people that might be otherwise hard to find.

- *ROI:* Adwords allows you to see exactly how many people clicked on your ad and then took your offer.

IDEA #4
Have a Facebook Business Page

It's no big secret that today's parents are massive users of social media and it's likely that in your market, 95% or more of them have a Facebook account. Facebook is the "800-pound gorilla" of social media sites and in my opinion you must be there. Moms are documenting their entire pregnancy and birth of their children on Facebook and using it as an online scrapbook. If your child care business does not have a Facebook business page (also called a "fan page") you are missing out on a huge source of qualified leads and traffic to your program.

Once you get your business account created, what should you do next? A great starting goal is to post updates – preferably including photos and videos – at least 3 times each week. People who are really "rocking it" are posting 1-2 times per day, usually around lunch time and then again around 4 pm. These are peak times for working moms to check in on their Facebook activity.

Page followers are currently measured by the number of "likes" your page has, so another important goal to track is

> **RESOURCE**
> • For a step-by-step training guide on Facebook, as well as Pinterest and LinkedIn, check out our Social Media 101 training course here: **www.childcare-marketing. com/social-media**

your number of likes. Ask all your existing parents to like your page, and put your Facebook page web address (URL) on all your marketing materials and in all email blasts you send out. For example, create a social media flyer in your prospect packet, and let people know how to connect with you on Facebook during the tour.

Finally, you should have a plan for increasing fan "engagement". You want people who like your page to interact with you. There are many ways to boost engagement: asking questions in a post (plain or peanut?), polls, and contests, among others. The more likes and engagement you build, the more that friends of your current moms and dads will see your posts and you will gain enrollment from the social relationship you've created. Get started!

IDEA #5
Be on Pinterest

As of the time I am writing this book (April 2014) Pinterest is an important and growing social media platform, especially for females in their 20's and 30's – AKA young moms. (Things can rapidly change in social media with mergers and acquisitions, and what's popular, so Pinterest may not be as important or even exist, in the future).

Think of Pinterest as an online "pin board" where users can pin images, pictures, quotes, and videos of stuff they love or are interested in. For example, if I'm really into raw foods, I may have a "pin" category for raw food recipes and pictures of yummy dishes. How does this apply to early childhood, you might be wondering. Moms are fans of your program will be very likely to "pin" cute pictures of kids including pictures of crafts, artwork, gardens, kids on group walking field trips, kids doing yoga, etc.

Similar to the Facebook strategy on the prior page, the first step is to go to Pinterest.com and create an account for your business. Once you have permission from parents to share images of their children online, you can start "pinning" cute photos, artwork, images, graphics of quotes, holiday-related ideas (like a picture of Cat in the Hat on Dr. Seuss's birthday on March 3), and the like. Search within Pinterest for "child care" or "preschool" to see what other programs are pinning, for ideas and inspiration.

You should be able to pin new images a few times each week and gain a following. This should only take about 20 minutes a week. You can also include a link in your pin, which could take people to your primary website, to your YouTube page, or to your Facebook page. Your goal is to create an online community of interested parents, and keep them engaged so you remain "top of mind". This is an easy task to delegate to a teacher or assistant director who wants more responsibility and loves social media.

IDEA #6
Have a YouTube Channel

Today's online marketing is hyper-focused on the use of video. Later in this book, I'll share my number one strategy for building your enrollment, and it involves video. (Hint: see page 84). The number one online video-sharing platform is YouTube. Moreover, YouTube is owned by Google, so having a YouTube channel and posting relevant content there will help you show up on Google for your top keywords. It's a win-win!

So how do you get started? First, ask your staff for help. What kind of videos can you and your team create, that will show off your program and communicate your unique benefits? Here are some thought-starters:

- Brief, unscripted video testimonials from parents and teachers – and even school-age kids.

- "FAQ" style videos – common questions parents ask about child care, and the answers.

- An "overview" tour video of your program, including its unique features and benefits.

- Parenting tips and other educational content on video.

- "Roving reporter" style videos from an event, such as a family carnival at your center.

Next, how to create the videos? What equipment do you need? The basic package of what you need: an iPhone or iPad as your camera, along with easy video editing software such as iMovie. The advanced package includes a Sony video camera and Sony Vegas editing software. If you capture a solid video, you don't even need to edit it.

Finally, once you have a couple videos "in the can", go to YouTube.com and create your channel. You just need to register with a login ID and password. Ideally, the name of your channel will reflect the name of your child care program and be easy to remember, and not too lengthy.

IDEA #7
Changeable Text Signage

As consumers who tend to travel similar routes during the week, we often suffer from "blindness" to ads or messages we see over and over again. You may have what you consider a great sign out front, but it may not be catching the attention of repeat drivers-by. The solution to this is to use what I call a "changeable text" sign. See a couple examples below.

These signs are extremely affordable (usually under $200), and they are likely to bring you many new enrollments if used right. The key is to vary your message, at least weekly. Tie your message into a holiday (or oddball holiday – see Page 100 for more on this). Promote a special you're running. Talk about new upcoming programs or seasonal changes in your program, such as your new and improved summer camp. Make it fun, and change it up for maximum effect.

One former client of mine with a Montessori school used a newsworthy message that tied in beautifully. Back in 2009, when Google stock prices were just starting to skyrocket, she posted on her changeable text sign:

> **"Google founders went to Montessori preschool. Let us help your child grow to their potential today! Stop in for a tour."**

This creative use of signage led to at least 5 new enrollments for this preschool. Now it's your turn.

IDEA #8
Online Reviews

Reviews and testimonials are one of the top strategies I teach my clients and members of my Child Care Success Academy. Most of them, before meeting me, have no reviews or testimonials online (either on their website or on review sites). They just don't understand the POWER of another human being, and preferably *many* of them, singing their praises. It's really all about TRUST. At the end of the day, the program that feels the most trustworthy to a parent will win the enrollment. Regardless of price or location, in most cases. Consider these stats: 82 percent of people consult online reviews to determine if a local business is a good business. And 72 percent of people trust online reviews as much as a personal recommendation.*(Source: ReviewBuzz)*

What's the best way to get started generating online reviews of your program? Have a little system in place. Make a plan to ask 5 parents every other week, for example, and send them an email with a direct link to where you want them to write the review online. This is effective because Google and other search engines like a steady, consistent stream of reviews rather a huge lump of them all at once. It feels more "real" and more credible.

If just 2 of those 5 parents in the above example actually post a review for you, your program will accumulate 48 reviews in one year. That is an incredible level of "social proof" that you do a great job, and it's almost irrefutable. In fact, I don't know of many child care programs with more than 20 reviews – so doing this one thing will really set your program apart online.

With that amount of happy reviews, even an occasional negative review will have little power. That's where you want to be. A strong and positive online reputation is worth gold for your program. Even if a disgruntled employee acts out online against you, it will have little weight and power with so many positives. That would feel great, right?

IDEA #9
Write a Book

The people in any industry who are perceived as authority-experts are ALWAYS higher paid than others. Throw a dash of "local celebrity" in the mix and you will command the highest fees or rates. Early childhood owners are typically very reluctant to "toot their own horn", let alone appear on local radio or TV as an education expert.

One of the best ways to get authority-expert status is to write a book. After all, the word "authority" has author within it, and that's no mistake. After I wrote my first book, my status (as well as my consulting fees) skyrocketed within the child care space. I was seen as an instant authority and had MUCH higher credibility.

If you want to charge higher rates – and be instantly trusted by parents who are considering enrolling with you – get started writing a book. It doesn't have to be lengthy – it could be a *Parents Survival Guide to Toddlers* and be 50 pages long. My client Beth Davis wrote a great book called *You Are Never Too Small to Make a Big Difference*, based on her early childhood approach and the philosophy of her school. (Learn more about Beth and how the book has changed her business on the next page).

These days, it's very easy and affordable to self-publish your book. One way is to write your book and use a self-publishing platform called CreateSpace. CreateSpace easily integrates with Amazon, so your book will be printed "on demand" and shipped out to buyers without you doing any extra work. You just collect a check. It's that easy. In fact, the book you are holding right now was published this way.

Alternately, if your book idea would appeal to early educators or administrators, as well as parents, you could approach an early childhood "niche" publisher such as Redleaf Press (the publisher of my first book) or Corwin Press. They'll provide an editor and publish your book, and you just collect a royalty check.

Idea #9: Write a Book

CASE STUDY:

Beth Davis,
Kids for Kids Academy

Beth Davis is the owner/director of her school and a recently published author of the book *"You are Never Too Small to Make a Big Difference."* She wrote the book because she wanted to impact families and children with her special message of positivity, kindness, and empowerment.

Beth leverages her author/expert status by giving a free copy of her book to everyone after they tour her school. Here is an excerpt about Beth from the foreword of her book, written by author Dianne Collins:

> One thing I can tell you for sure - Beth is the real deal. Now, as with anyone who has truly mastered an area of life, Beth Davis offers the priceless value of her experience to all of us in this precious gem that every parent and teacher should read together with their kids. We learn together that through simple acts of kindness we transform adversities into miracles of love, of commitment and connection. By teaching our children well, we create a better world. As Beth states with genuine matter-of-fact flair, "You are never too small to make a big difference." You are never too big to make that difference either.

Based on this level of professional experience and positive impacts on children, it's obvious that the book provides Beth with instant credibility and authority as an expert on child development. So who would you rather have as the owner/director of your child's learning experience – Beth Davis or some unknown "Jane Doe"? I'll pick Beth.

Resource Links:
Learn more about Beth Davis and her book at www.teachkidskindess.com.
Learn more about her school at www.kidsforkidsacademy.com

IDEA #10
Start a Blog

If writing a book seems too daunting, or just isn't appealing to you, how about starting a blog? A blog is a great way to "dip your toe" in the water of authorship, one easy article at a time.

Your blog should contain articles of interest to your target market. Yes, your target market is parents of young children, but what else is specifically of interest to your specific market? A parent living in a large urban area is likely to have different interests than one in a rural farmland area.

Furthermore, what are your specific areas of expertise and interest? In the previous case study, Beth Davis could blog about the key ideas in her book, and how they apply to today's child and family. Another great way to gain interest in your blog is to write about what's in the news, trends, issues, even stuff that's controversial. It's okay to have a point of view and people will generally respect you for it, even if they disagree.

For ideas, look around the internet and see what other "mommy blogs" and child care blogs contain. You'll likely get inspired and gain some great ideas.

The logistics of setting up a blog are simple. Just get a Wordpress account and link it to your main website. Your webmaster (or you) can add a button or tab to your main website navigation menu that says "Blog" or "Articles". You'll then want to create categories that match what you're likely to write about, such as "Parenting", "Education", "How-To Craft Projects", etc. Happy blogging!

IDEA #11
Create a "Lead Magnet"

What is a lead magnet? Also sometimes referred to as an "irresistible free offer" or IFO, a lead magnet is something you offer for free to your prospects in order to initiate a relationship with them. Usually a lead magnet is offered in exchange for someone's contact information, such as first name and email address.

It's based on the idea that in today's world, it's harder than ever to get the first sale. People are less trusting than ever before in the history of our economy – especially when they are going to trust someone with their precious child.

A lead magnet helps your prospect get to <u>know</u> you, <u>like</u> you, and <u>trust</u> you BEFORE they ever give you any money (or before they enroll). The good news is: even though lead magnets such as special reports, white papers, checklists, videos, webinars, and free books are being used widely in many different industries, very few early childhood businesses are using lead magnets. I'd bet money that none (or maybe one) of your key competitors is using a lead magnet on their website.

Moreover, lead magnets are a great way to build your "house list" (see Idea #1). They allow you to build relationships and trust with people. They increase your word of mouth, as friends sometimes share them with each other *("Oh hey, you're looking for a preschool? Let me send you this cool checklist I got from ABC Academy...")*

Get started by creating a free report, checklist, consumer guide, or video series that educates your ideal client. Then use an email management system such as Mail Chimp, AWeber, Constant Contact, or iContact to start building your list.

Idea #11: Create a Lead Magnet

CASE STUDY:

Kevin and Becky Patrick,
A Child's Academy

Kevin & Becky Patrick

When Kevin and Becky came on board to help increase the enrollment and profitability of their family-owned child care center, they knew that one of the first things smart marketers do is "build a list". So they set out to create a couple different lead magnets that they could put on their website and drive prospects to opt in with name and email.

The first lead magnet they created was a free report called "The 16 Must-Know Things about How to Choose the Best Preschool".

They also created an email "drip campaign" that would automatically send relationship-building emails with valuable content to the person after they opted in, over a period of several weeks.

The free report worked well, but they kept getting inquiry calls from people asking for tuition rates. So Kevin decided to test a "Rates and Info Packet" as his lead magnet. This packet massively outperformed the free report, with a 20% overall opt-in rate in the first 6 months versus the free report which got a 2-3% opt-in rate.

In the first two years of using lead magnets on their home page, Kevin and Becky built an email list of 4,483 people in the Gainesville area, most of whom are high-quality families seeking child care. Today, their list size has grown to approximately 9,500. Now, their enrollment is full and they've added a second location. This is in large part due to being able to market to their list, whenever they have something valuable, promotional, or newsworthy to communicate.

Resource Link:
For more information on A Child's Academy, visit www.achildsacademy.com

IDEA #12
Write Articles for Local Media

Other than writing a book, there's no better way to create an "expert persona" for yourself than being seen in local media as an authority. Many local newspapers, magazines, and websites are always seeking new sources of content. Because you're an expert on young children, you can offer a unique perspective. Or maybe you own more than one type of business and you'd like to write articles on what it's like to own small businesses on "Main Street" in your town.

Simply approach the editors of your local publications and ask them if they are looking for fresh content. You could write a monthly article, or just provide one occasionally.

Idea #13
Sign Up for Online Directories

There are dozens of websites, called directories, that list businesses in every category you can imagine. Most of them are free. Here's a list of early childhood-related directories you can list your business in:

Angie's List

Greatschools.org

CareLuLu

Care.com

SavvySource

InsiderPages.com

Yelp.com

Superpages

Manta

Citysearch

YellowPages

Foursquare

eLocal

DaycareBear

DaycareMatch

Daycare.com

MasterMOZ

Craigslist

Idea #14
Create a Consumer Awareness Guide

One type of "lead magnet" is a Consumer Awareness Guide. People are naturally attracted to this type of resource, because the very title suggests that there are "secrets" we don't know about a certain topic that we should be aware of.

Within your guide, you could include many ideas and resources for parents that they probably don't know. For example, you could include the "5 Factors that Determine Quality Child Care" published by the National Association of Child Care Referral Agencies (NACCRA). You could include the latest "quality indicators" from your state. You could do a chapter all about your state subsidy programs and how to qualify.

The point is, to provide a fresh perspective on early childhood factors and decision-making, based on what you uniquely know as an expert in the field, and what your program uniquely offers.

Here are some links to articles you may want to review and/or get permission to reprint in your Consumer Awareness Guide (note that as these web pages age, they may no longer be available):

http://www.childcareaware.org/parents-and-guardians/child-care-101

http://www.childcareaware.org/parents-and-guardians/helpful-tools

http://www.childcareaware.org/parents-and-guardians/resources

http://centerforparentingeducation.org/library-of-articles

http://www.care.com/child-care-articles

Plus, you can Google "child care articles for parents" or "child care tools for parents" and get more!

Idea #15
Market to Local Mom's Clubs

Most towns and cities have "moms clubs" that act as social groups and educational resources for moms of young children. My former town had a group called "Preschool Parents" with over 150 members. About half of these moms were stay-at-home and half were working. This club brought in a speaker once a month, on a parenting or family-related topic, and they were always seeking fresh speakers. They also sponsored local family events such as carnivals in the park and preschool fairs. Obviously, this would be a natural fit for you to engage and promote your program.

The first step is to contact your Chamber of Commerce, school administrative board, or PTA, and find out if there are any parenting or moms groups in your area, focused on preschoolers. Then, make a connection with those groups. Let them know you have resources that could help them (such as the Consumer Guide mentioned on the prior page) and find out if there are opportunities for you to be a speaker at or sponsor of one of their events.

Idea #16
Run Facebook Contests

Once your Facebook business page is up and running, your next challenge is to grow the number of fans or "likes" on your page. One of the very best ways to do this quickly is to run a contest. When you get parents to compete with one another, you can get great results.

One effective contest idea is the "vote for your favorite door" contest. Teachers decorate the front doors of their classroom based on a certain theme or holiday (Thanksgiving, or Super Bowl, for example) and parents are asked to go "vote" on the photo of the door that's their favorite. Any parent who also "likes" the overall Facebook page will be entered into a drawing for a fun and valuable prize.

Another Facebook contest idea is to do a simple giveaway drawing for anyone who "Likes" your page during a given timeframe (click like, enter your name & email, and be entered into a drawing for an iPad). It's good to run these contests for about 7 days – long enough to gain traction and give everyone a chance to enter, but not too long that it loses steam.

Many center owners or directors who are my clients have done this contest and received 100-300 new "likes" (or more) on their main Facebook page. You don't need to limit it to existing client families – you can also promote the contest to your alumni families and prospective families who are on your list.

Idea #16: Facebook Contests

CASE STUDY:

Mary Wardlaw,
The Children's Center

Our most successful Facebook contest is our "Door Decorating Contest". We do this every quarter, and we tie it to seasonal themes. Teachers and their students in each classroom are responsible for decorating their classroom door. I love this contest because the teachers' creativity really comes out, they take pride in how their doors look

Mary Wardlaw

and touring families get a great first impression of the school.

The idea is to have people "like" our page then vote on their favorite classroom door. Parents and staff get very involved and our likes rapidly increase!

We went from 80 likes to over 600 in the last year - mostly because of the 4 contests we've run. The winning classroom gets $100 of new toys and materials picked by the teacher.

Here are 4 photos of actual doors from these contests:

Resource Link:
To learn more about Mary Wardlaw and The Children's Center, please visit
www.NilesKids.Com

Idea #17
Map It Out

Here's an exercise that will provide a new level of clarity about the "sweet spots" in your community that you draw your best clients from.

Get a regional map and lay it out on a large table. Using a highlighter, mark your location on the map.

Use a black pen to mark the home address (if your business is residentially located) or work address (if your business is commercially located) of every parent enrolled with you. Consider using a different color pen or even colored push pins to note work versus home addresses.

Identify your sweet spots—the neighborhoods and commercial areas that are a natural geographic fit for your program.

Mark the location of all your competitors—early childhood programs, preschools, and family child cares homes alike. Your local CCR&R can provide you with a complete listing.

Look for new and upcoming pockets of opportunity—new housing developments, new businesses, new construction sites, and so on.

Idea #18
Track What's Working (ROI)

What are the top 3 advertising methods you use to make your phone ring? Do you know? When I ask this question to many owners and leaders, I get either "I have no clue" or "I *think*…". In order to have full and *accurate* clarity about where you should spend more ad dollars (and where you should stop spending) you must track not only how many overall inquiries you are getting each month, but how they are finding you.

There are 3 ways to track what's making your phone ring:

1) Ask. Simply ask every single time, "how did you hear about us", then dig more deeply if you need to for clarification.

2) Promo codes. Use a special promo code on an ad, web page, flyer, or mailer to identify that specific campaign.

3) Tracking phone numbers. See Idea 19 on the next page.

Taking it one step further, once you gather accurate data on how specific prospects are finding you, you can track which ones turn into enrollments. Based on the average revenue one enrollment brings your program, you can then determine the return-on-investment (ROI) of that specific media, promotion, or campaign.

For example, say you spent $750 on print ads in "Family Times" local magazine in second quarter. Based on the promo code you used in the ad, you determine that you received just 1 new enrollment from that campaign, which on average brings $7,500 of enrollment revenue to your program per year. So your year 1 return on investment for that campaign is 10x, or for every dollar you spent, you brought 10 in. If that family stays with you for 3 or 4 years, your ROI would be much greater.

Based on a comparison of the ROI of different media and campaigns, you can determine which you want to continue or increase, and which you want to discontinue or tweak. This is a much more numbers-based and strategic approach than what I call "throw it against the wall and see what sticks" marketing.

Idea #19
Use a Phone Tracking System

There are companies who can provide you with local tracking phone numbers and a complete report on how many calls came into those numbers. This is the 100% fool-proof method to get the best data and it's usually very affordable.

What's more, these systems enable you to record every inbound phone call, so you can listen back to what parents are asking and saying. You can also use the recordings as a training tool for staff – and a way to hold staff accountable to behave on the telephone the way you want them to.

RESOURCE

For help with using a block of local phone tracking numbers, I recommend a company called New Call Solutions. Learn more at: **www.newcallsolutions. com**

Direct Mail Ideas

Idea #20
Mother's Day Cards

If you're a Mom, wouldn't it be nice to get a Mother's Day card from a local business where you're a frequent customer – such as your hair salon? Would it make you feel more "warm and fuzzy" about that business? Would you tell your girlfriends about it, or even post about it on social media? Would it make you happy to keep doing business there?

The answer of course, is a resounding Yes. And what better business to build relationships with Moms than a learning center or preschool. It's a natural fit.

It's a good idea to send these cards to your existing clients as well as prospects. For prospects, you may opt to include a special "Mothers Day" enrollment offer, or summer camp offer, in with the card.

> **RESOURCE**
> Have you heard of a service called Send Out Cards? You can easily send out cards any time of year using this done-for-you system. Just create an account, import your mailing list, and create your own personalized cards – they do the fulfillment and mailing for you. Learn more at: **www. childcarecards.com**

Of course, Mother's Day is just the beginning. You can and should send cards throughout the year, for children's birthdays (see page 80) or many other holidays and reasons.

Idea #21
Use 3-D or "Lumpy" Mail

Have you ever received a package or letter in the mail that's 3-dimensional, or "lumpy"? It's clearly got something inside the envelope and just the sheer curiosity of the thing causes you to open it. What's more, you can't put the lumpy envelope at the bottom of the mail pile, because stuff won't stack on top of it! It's got to go on TOP of the pile, and even better - it's very likely to get opened immediately.

For this reason, I am a huge fan of lumpy mail. I use it with great results in my business, and many of my clients do too. So how can you use lumpy or 3-D mail?

> **RESOURCE**
> Learn more at: **www.childcare-marketing.com/3dmail**

There are lots of cute objects you can put in the mail, such as pacifiers, mini baby bottles and blankets, aspirin packets, worry dolls, small toys, hourglasses with sand, the list is almost endless.

The key is to tie in the 3-D object you are mailing with the message of the letter or mailer. For example, if you send a set of small worry dolls, the headline of your letter could be "We're Sending You These Worry Dolls So You Can Stop Worrying about the Care Your Child is Receiving, After You Enroll with Us."

My buddy Travis Lee at 3D Mail Results and I have put together a free pamphlet showing you some ways you can use these items to get your mail opened, and to get huge results. Just go to the link provided in the Resource box to get your free guide.

Idea #22
Mail a Children's Book

This is one of the most effective post-tour follow up ideas I know. Purchase several dozen children's books in different age-appropriate levels. You can get inexpensive books from Scholastic, the dollar store, eBay, or even Amazon.

After the tour, if the family does not enroll, put the book in a large white or colored envelope, addressed to the child. Insert a letter to the parents, letting them know how much you enjoyed meeting them and perhaps with a special limited-time offer to enroll.

Idea #23
Regularly Mail Prospects in Your "Best Neighborhoods"

I first heard about the best neighborhood strategy from sales and marketing expert Chet Holmes (www.chetholmes.com). Sadly, Chet passed away but his great ideas live on. The *best neighborhood strategy* helps you identify a market sweet spot based on where your best customers and your best prospects live or work so you can aggressively court these folks using direct marketing.

Examples of direct marketing include direct mail, door hangers, flyers hung on mailboxes, or even door-to-door visits. Think about it: if month after month you receive an interesting, fun mailer with a special offer from a restaurant near where you live or work, aren't you curious enough to check it out?

Likewise, if you consistently mail a fun, charming, money-saving offer to households with young children in your best neighborhood, then you will almost certainly have prospects from this neighborhood consistently calling about your program. The key is to mail slightly different pieces to your best neighborhood repeatedly—not once, not twice, but every month until they give in and give you a call!

Idea #24
Mail to New Movers

Give some logical thought to the decision process for families who need child care. Typically, people will seek child care for 3 main reasons:

- They had a job change / mom is going back to work

- They are dissatisfied with their current care arrangement (including leaving one of your competitors and coming to you)

- They are moving into the area

RESOURCE
You can buy lists of people who are "new movers" but you cannot select only households with children within these lists. However, because you know they are new and are likely to need child care, it's still a smart strategy that many are not using.
Get lists of new movers at:
www.InfoUSA.com

Therefore, doesn't it make sense to have a marketing plan that "speaks" to people in each of these situations? Or at the very least, to recognize the differences in the "inner conversation" going on with each of these folks, so you can build a relationship with them more effectively.

Here are some concrete and easy strategies for reaching the latter category, families moving into town.

- Advertise with Welcome Wagon

- Buy a list of new movers

- Target new housing developments and Model Homes

- Work with local realtors and offer a special promotion to their clients

- Promote within apartment complexes (get permission from the manager first)

- What else can you think of?

The Phone Inquiry

Idea #25
Make Sure a Human Can Always Be Reached During Business Hours

After years of field visits and mystery phone calling in this industry, it still astounds and saddens me that so many programs let so many enrollments and revenue slip through their fingers due to shoddy phone practices. While the phone is becoming slightly less utilized by prospects for the initial inquiry (email is on the rise), it's still one of the most important enrollment-building tools you have.

The best of all scenarios is to have your phone answered within 3 rings by a human being who's trained to be *and sound* cheerful, professional, and knowledgeable. This is the very first impression a prospective mom will get of your school, so it needs to right. A "wow" welcome makes a huge first impression – something like "let me be the first to welcome you to ABC Academy!".

Another acceptable phone-answering scenario is to have a warm but brief automated greeting followed by an easy to understand "phone tree" – press 1 if you're new to us and looking for enrollment information – press 2 if you're currently enrolled with us – etc. But if you use this option, you're going to want to be sure that a live human being is standing by at extension 1, ready to go – avoid the calls just dumping into voicemail at all costs. This is a sure-fire way to lose leads and prospective enrollments.

Idea #26
Use a Phone Script or "Cheat Sheet"

Has this ever happened to you? You pick up the phone and start speaking with a very interested prospective mom about your program. Within 10 seconds, a teacher shows up at your door in tears. Then the toilet overflows. Then a grandparent shows up to pick up a child early, and the parent gave you no advance warning. What do you do?

If you have a phone script, you will be much more likely to handle this situation with ease. A script is simply a tool or "cheat sheet" that allows you to put this process on auto-pilot in the face of distractions, a bout of forgetfulness, or simply a bad day.

> **RESOURCE**
> We have a tested, tried, and proven phone success script that we give to our members of the Child Care Success Academy, with ongoing training and role-play. Learn more about the Academy at:
> **www.childcare-marketing. com/success-academy**

The script should contain 5 parts:

- The "wow" welcome
- The "discovery" and rapport-building phase
- Communication of your program's differences
- Booking the tour or visit
- The close

The goal of every prospect phone call is two-fold. One, you should get the tour booked. Second, you should gain the caller's contact information, so you can follow up with them effectively, especially if they choose not to book the tour or they don't show up for the tour. The script allows you to effectively get at least one of these goals met, if not both, 100 percent of the time. You are no longer "winging it" but demonstrating confidence, competence, and consistency to your callers.

Best of all, they will get off the phone thinking to themselves "wow, that was different – and refreshing!"

Idea #26: Use a Phone Script

CASE STUDY:

Don Sutton,
Crowned Hart Preschools

Don Sutton is the owner of four schools in St. Augustine, Florida. Like many preschool owners, he managed just fine for years without a website, social media, or any sales skills or tools for his staff. He didn't really know how much revenue he was leaving on the table until he started implementing many of the "Kris Murray" ideas in this book.

Don Sutton

Perhaps the most powerful of all is his team's use of the phone script. The script allows his team to immediately set themselves apart from all other centers, build rapport with the caller, have a way to not give rates over the phone, and to more effectively book the visit, every time.

This is what Don has to say about the phone script along with the specific results his program has gotten from using it:

"The phone script has worked great for all our schools. The phone script allows us to make that connection with the parent immediately. We start building the relationship immediately, by getting the child's name, age and likes. Once this relationship and rapport has been established with the parent on the phone, it is easy to get the pertinent information including the e-mail address to stay in contact with them.

We set the tour, send out an e packet, and get their word they will call us if they cannot make the appointment. Then we text them an hour before appointment to say we are looking forward to meeting them. This has really reduced our tour no-shows.

Since using the phone script that Kris taught us, we have increased our enrollments and the quality of the customer. (We no longer get many who are shopping just on price). Our directors/staff who were not comfortable on the phone now get the information with ease and already have a rapport with the parent when they come in. The phone script is a definite game changer."

Resource Link: To learn more about Don Sutton and his program, visit www.CrownedHartPreschools.com

Idea #27
Certify Your Staff on the Script and Phone Process

Now that you have a phone script in place, you want to not only train your staff on how to use it, but you want an actual certification process in place. This way, any team member who is not "certified" to meet your more rigorous standards will be authorized to do a full prospect phone call.

One of my clients certifies his team members through monthly training and role-play sessions, and when they feel confident, they role-play with the owner who acts as a prospective dad caller. If they can effectively follow the script and show they understand the phone protocol, they gain certification.

Now let's talk about your phone "process". More than just the words being communicated through the script or cheat-sheet, you should have a phone process that ensures 100% capture of every prospect or lead. That could be a software system, a spreadsheet, or a binder with Prospect Information Forms inside. What it should *not* be is a bunch of yellow sticky notes all over the desk or computer. Invariably, these leads will get lost and they are nearly impossible to follow up with in any effective and trackable manner.

Idea #28
Don't Give Rates over the Phone

Recently, I've been warning about the increased "commoditization" of child care. That is, increasingly parents seem to be hyper-aware of rates and choosing child care based on rates and location, rather than value, unique benefits, and differences from one program to the next.

Why is this? Part of the problem is that we are doing a poor job educating parents about what's really important: quality, ratios, accreditations, teacher experience and energy, nutrition, and things like what "developmentally appropriate" really means (and why they should care).

When you immediately give your rates out over the phone, then fail to communicate any of the above value points, you do a disservice not only to parents seeking care but also to children and teachers in your community. Ideally, you can "re-direct" the conversation by telling the caller "I can help you with that" and then continuing on to lead the conversation in the direction you want it to go.

See the next page, Idea 29, for an effective way to avoid giving your rates over the phone while gaining the contact information for the prospect so you can follow up with him or her.

You can also offer to share the rates during the tour. Say something like "our rates are competitive and we'd like to share the full array of pricing options with you when you come visit."

Idea #29
Offer to Send an E-Packet with Rates

What's an e-Packet? It's my invention – a way for my clients to share information and rates with prospects, while at least getting something in return: the prospect's name and email address. (You may also then offer to mail a package of info to their home address and thereby obtain the mailing address of their home, which will be very useful as you build your "house list").

When prospects ask for your rates over the phone, I recommend first offering to share the rates during the *tour*. Say something like "our rates are competitive and we'd like to share the full array of pricing options with you when you come visit."

If they're not ready to book the visit, then offer the e-Packet. You might name it something jazzy like "our Parent Info Packet." Here's how to language it:

> *"Rather than just quoting you the rate, I'm going to do something special for you. We have a super-informative Parent Resource Packet that includes our rates along with 5 pages of info and a child care checklist. What's your email address and I'll send it right over. I can even stay on the line with you to make sure it arrives in your in-box."*

What to include in your e-Packet? Below are some ideas. Just compile it, save it as a PDF, and you're ready to go.

- Story from the Owner

- Letter from the Director

- Teacher Bio's / Experience

- Unique Benefits / Unique Value Statement

- Written Parent Testimonials (with full name and photo if you can)

- Rate Sheet

- Parent Articles

- Tips for Choosing the Right Child Care

- Child Care Checklist

- Reprints of Local Media Coverage (i.e. Interview in Local Paper)

- Q&A with Teachers or Owner

Idea #30
Always Ask Prospects to Book a Tour

Again, the goal of every prospect phone call is two-fold. First and foremost, you want to get the tour booked. Second, you should gain the caller's contact information, so you can follow up with them effectively, especially if they choose not to book the tour or they don't show up for the tour.

The mistake I often see being made is an offer to send the e-Packet as the end goal of the call, rather than giving the caller a reason and motivation to want to come visit your program.

For most of my clients, it costs about $75 to $100 in marketing dollars to get the phone to ring one time. You can figure this out by tracking how many calls you get per quarter versus how much you're spending in marketing. When you don't book the visit, and you don't get the contact information from the caller, it's like flushing that money down the toilet.

Idea #31
Give an Incentive to Book the Tour

So now you know how much you're losing by not booking the tour… how do you motivate callers to come visit? Offer them an incentive. Offer a free children's book with each tour. Have "Family Tote Bags" created with toys, books, promotional offers, etc. Promote the value of your tote bag, book, or other freebie as a way to incentivize callers.

The other great strategy is to use the "law of scarcity" as a motivator. When you discover that there's only "one time slot left" for something you are interested in, it makes you want it more, right? This is the law of scarcity in play. Tell prospects that you have just 2 available openings for tours this week – Wednesday at 10 or Friday at 3, and which would they prefer. The likelihood of them choosing one of those "scarce" slots is very high – much higher than just leaving it open-ended or saying "just come in any time".

Idea #32
Eliminate Tour No-Shows

Have you had a parent book a tour at your child care center, only to not show up when it's time for the tour? It happens a lot in our industry; parents are busy and forget, or decide on another child care option. However, it is a big time waster for you and your business, and there are actions you can take to prevent this from happening. I have two strategies you can use to virtually eliminate enrollment tour no-shows.

First is to choose the closing language of your phone conversation very carefully. I recommend saying something such as, "Now we realize emergencies happen and things can come up in your schedule. Could you please do me a favor and give us a call if something comes up so that we can reschedule." Then pause. Give them the chance to say yes and create a verbal contract with you.

They will be much less likely to no-show if you frame it right from the beginning that they are expected to call you if their plans change. You can also say something along the lines of, "We have a lot of parents calling us to book tours and we'd love to be able to provide that slot to someone else if your plans do change." This creates a sense of scarcity at your program and makes it all that more desirable. Just this one strategy will help you reduce tour no-shows by at least 30-40%.

The other strategy is to send a reminder to the parents. Towards the end of the conversation you can let them know you would like to offer them the service of a text reminder or an email reminder that you can send an hour before the tour. This also provides the opportunity to get or verify their phone and email if you haven't done so already. Then you also have permission to text the parent which also provides another opportunity for follow-up after the tour.

Idea #33
Build Trust and Rapport

The idea of building trust and rapport with your prospects is a massive one. If you master it, you will stay full with a waiting list. It's what today's parents want in every purchase decision they make: to know, like, and trust the people they do business with. This is *especially* true when it comes to decisions regarding the well-being (and future success) of their children.

So how do you go about building trust and rapport with prospects on the phone? One strategy is called "pre-framing" and it's based on what prospects read and hear about you, even before they pick up the phone. Your school is "pre-framed" by your online reputation – reviews, testimonials, the quality of your website, the number of "likes" you have on social media, etc. When you work on improving your online reputation and social proof, your inquiries will grow because people will be more likely to call based on positive word of mouth, even if it's from strangers online.

The next step is to answer your phone with a live human who's friendly, engaging, professional and knowledgeable. That's a huge step for trust in the right direction. If I get an answering machine, I may not call back because my trust instinct has been questioned. So all that pre-framing work you did was a sheer waste of effort.

Finally, use your phone script to engage the caller. For example, use their name and their child's name, repeatedly but in a natural way. People love the sound of their names and it's almost magical in building rapport. Ask them to tell you about their child. What are Molly's interests? Any parenting challenges? Are they new to the neighborhood? Are congratulations in order? Be interested in them, rather than just giving your "schpiel".

Conducting Effective Tours

Idea #34
Maximize Your Curb Appeal

When's the last time you really looked at your curb appeal with a fresh eye? When you drive by your school or center, versus your competitors, what does the curb appeal of each really tell you?

Your curb appeal needs to serve you in a couple ways. At the very basic level, it needs to communicate that you're a business that cares about its customers – families and young children. At a more sophisticated level, it needs to match your "brand" and what you stand for. Here are some specific things you can look for, when comparing your curb appeal to that of your competitors:

- Is the signage clearly visible and in good repair?

- Is the landscaping updated, maintained, and neat?

- Is the playground in good repair and free of debris?

- Are the exteriors and fences free of debris and peeling paint?

- How could this facility and grounds be improved to look more up-to-date, appealing, and upscale?

- What impressions do you get from looking at the curb appeal of this school?

Idea #35
Make a Great First Impression

You may have heard this phrase: "you only have about 7 seconds to make a good first impression".But have you really thought about what that means in context of your child care tour?

There are 5 elements key to creating an excellent first impression:

- **Personal Appearance.** A professional appearance is extremely important to a great first impression. Whoever is conducting your tours should be well-groomed, dressed nicely (or at least "business casual" and attractive), and have attractive footwear that's in good condition.

- **Verbal Greeting.** Introduce yourself to the prospect, including your full name and your position or role in your program. Parents want the context of the organization, so if you're the assistant director, say so – and be sure to introduce the parent to the director if she or he is on site. If you're also the owner, say so! Don't be shy or timid – be direct and confident!

- **Smile.** People will remember how you made them feel during the tour, more than what you said. So exude an easy confidence and optimistic nature. The best way to do that is a simple warm smile.

- **Handshake.** Shake hands with your prospect when you greet them for the first time (accompanied by your smile and your verbal greeting). Give a firm handshake, but not overly firm. This is a signal of professionalism and confidence.

- **Preparedness.**

> *"By failing to prepare, you are preparing to fail."*
> – Benjamin Franklin

A big part of asking parents to schedule a tour with you (rather than just showing up any time) is to allow you to *be prepared*. Remind the lead teacher of the prospective child's room that a tour will be by in 10 minutes. Gather your Parent Questionnaire and tour packet. Make sure your gift or goodie bag is ready (see page 49 for more on this idea). Be prepared, ready, and confident!

Idea #36
Address the Five Senses

During your tour, you need to take all 5 senses into account, as part of making a fantastic initial impression on your prospect. Work towards creating a strategic plan to "wow" your prospect in each area. Here are some suggestions for how to do this:

- Smell: This is one of the most important sensory experiences, especially for women. Go outside and get a fresh "nose" then come back inside your environment. What do you smell? Is it positive, negative, or neutral? How can you enhance the smell consistently, so it's always positive – even inside the infant room at the end of the day?

- Sight: What do people see as they drive up to your school? Is your curb appeal positive, and how does it compare to your competitors? Can you enhance your curb appeal with flowers, better signage, and/or other improvements? What about the inside of the building? As they enter, are there engaging things to look at, without being too "busy"?

- Sound: I recommend you have some soft music playing in the lobby of your program (or in your family child care home) to set the tone for a fun learning environment. You can choose classical, soft jazz, spa music, Disney soundtracks, or whatever suits you – just make sure it's a calming influence on what can be a hectic drop-off and pick-up experience. You want your prospects and customers to feel as if they've come in to a "safe haven" away from the stresses of the outside world.

- Taste: One great way to set yourself apart from other programs is to offer snacks and beverages to your visitors. When people are offered coffee, tea, water, and healthy snacks (for both parents and child) it reminds people of visiting a friend's home.

- Touch: Create a warm, comfortable environment for your prospect to sit and get to know you better. Provide a child-size table and chairs with books, toys, and crayons for the child. Don't make the mistake of starting and ending the tour "standing up at the counter." You'll engender much more trust and make a deeper connection with your prospect if you provide a comfy place to sit.

Idea #37
Do a Parent Interview / Needs Assessment

This is one of the most important parts of your tour, and a step that is often missed or skipped. It's something I call the "interactive needs assessment". This technique allows you to make an emotional connection with your prospect, and enables you to really understand (and be able to respond to) what I call his or her "hot buttons". Your goal during the tour is to really understand the fears, concerns, past experiences, desires, and objections of your prospect – so you can address them and be better prepared to ask for the enrollment at the end of the visit.

The best way to elegantly handle this relationship-building technique is by using a Prospect Questionnaire and walking through it as an interactive 'chit-chat' – if you leave the room and have Mom or Dad complete it on their own, you've missed an opportunity to build rapport, trust, and shared understanding. Plus, you'll have a less clear understanding of his or her "hot buttons".

Create your Prospect Questionnaire and include open-ended questions that provide insight into the parent's fears, concerns, past experiences, desires, and objections. Good ones to ask may include "what are your goals for your child over the next 4 years", "do you have concerns about Kindergarten readiness", and "tell me about any parenting challenges you have and how we can help".

You will find that 95% of other child care programs do not take the time to conduct this assessment. If you do, not only will you set yourself apart, you will be seen as more caring and trustworthy than others.

Idea #38
Facilitate the Parent-Teacher Conversation (Bonding)

Think about this. The child care decision is perhaps the most *trust-based* decision anyone can make in terms of a product or service. So whatever you can do during your center tour to enhance the sense of trust will bring you one step closer to securing the enrollment.

Now, think about how you orchestrate the greeting and bond between parent and teacher, during the visit. Do you take over the classroom briefly, so the parent and teacher can visit? Does the teacher greet each parent visitor with a smile and a firm handshake? This behavior conveys the highest level of professionalism, and makes a fantastic impression with parents. Every teacher in your program is an important "selling tool" for your school, and they need to be trained and motivated to help secure that enrollment.

Of course, some teachers will be natural enrollment-builders more than others. It's your job to enable the communication to flow and bonds to take place, by training teachers what to say, offering to role-play, providing encouragement and incentives, and praising teachers when they do a good job.

Idea #39
Give a Gift or Goodie Bag

Dr. Robert Cialdini studied the psychology of influence (and selling) and wrote the book *Influence: The Psychology of Persuasion*. One of the top influencers is what Cialdini calls "the law of reciprocity". This means that when people are given a gift or done a favor, they feel compelled (guilt plays a role) to reciprocate the good deed.

And your program can set itself apart by giving a fun and/or educational gift to each family who takes the time to visit you. Again, 90% of child care organizations do NOT use this technique – do you want to stand out among the crowd?

So what should be included in your gift package or goodie bag? First, I recommend including some items branded with your school's logo, which find their way into the prospect's home. These can include mugs, sippy cups, chip clips, children's clothing, onesies, bibs, or hats.

You can also include educational items such as children's books, educational toys, or crafts. Inexpensive fillers like bubbles and crayons can be found at the dollar store, and can bring great glee from both parents and children.

Now that you have your goodie bag (or package of inexpensive Scholastic books tied in a ribbon) pulled together, you should have one at the ready for each visit. Give the gift near the end of the visit, right before you ask for the enrollment. This will ease any nervousness on your part, and engender feelings of goodwill among all parties.

Idea #39: Give a Gift or Goodie Bag

CASE STUDY:

Gerry Pastor & Jane Porterfield, Educational Playcare

The idea of giving a gift or "goodie bag" during your tour is based on the Law of Reciprocity. This means that when you receive a gift or favor from someone, you are much more likely to want to reciprocate and do a kindness for that person. It also builds the "like and trust" factor with that person. Furthermore, you are much more likely to remember that person (and their business) because the sheer act of giving set them apart in your mind.

For all those reasons, it's a very smart (and heartwarming) idea to give a gift or goodie bag at the end of your tour, immediately prior to asking mom or dad for their business.

What should be inside your goodie bag? Here is an example of the exact bag and contents given by Educational Playcare at all 6 of their locations. Gerry and Jane have invested time and effort to include a childen's book along with six logo'd items: a tote bag, to-go mug, onesie (or child's t-shirt depending on the age of the child in the family who's taking the tour), freezer penguin for boo-boo's, band-aid dispenser, and a pen (not shown).

Resource Link: Learn more about Educational Playcare at www.EducationalPlaycare.com

Idea #40
Ask for the Enrollment

Okay, I know what you're thinking….

"I don't want to be sales-y."

"I'm scared of rejection. What if they say no?"

"I don't think selling is appropriate in child care."

I'm not asking you to be a used car salesman, not even close. What I am asking you is to be a leader. Lead your prospect to where you *know* their child will be served – in your program. It's actually your duty to let them know you want them. And they want to be wanted.

So your job here is to close the tour by bringing them back to your office (or that quiet comfy place we mentioned earlier) and let them know you think their child would be a great fit in Miss Janie's room. That you would like to sign them up, so you can ease their mind, and reduce their stress around this important decision.

Ease their pain – solve their problem. It's that simple. Create and practice language that you feel comfortable with. You could say something as simple as "we think Holly would really thrive in Miss Janie's room. When would you like to start?" Whatever language you choose, be sure to close the tour by asking for the enrollment.

Idea #41
Have a Multi-Media Follow-Up Campaign

In today's digital age, studies have shown it takes a minimum of 7 "touches" with a new company in order for someone to feel comfortable doing business with them. This is because we as a society are less trusting than we used to be, and we want to build a relationship with people before we trust them with our dollars – or our children. I have a strong feeling you are not doing much follow-up after the tour at all, let alone 7 touches. Am I right?

Listen, people may not be ready to enroll at the point they come for a tour. Perhaps they are just in the "info gathering" phase. Or maybe they just found out they are pregnant with their first child. Either way, you need a system for following up that reaches them in multiple methods: phone, email, snail mail, maybe text – you might even in-mail them through Facebook or LinkedIn.

If you're not following up, in multi-media methods, you are leaving serious enrollments and money on the table. Here's a sample campaign you might implement:

- Day 1 after tour: Mail book to child's home with parent letter

- Day 3: Phone call with cute message if goes to voicemail/machine

- Day 5: Email "thinking about you"

- Day 7: Hand-written note or Greeting Card mailed to home

- Day 10: Phone Call

- Day 13: Email #2

- Day 16: Email #3

- Day 20: Email #4

Idea #41: Have a Multi-Media Follow-Up System

CASE STUDY:
Annette Gentry,
Creative Day School

Annette and her team have proven that the "for-tune" really is in the follow-up. Over the past six months, Annette has extended her follow-up cam-paign to include at least seven initial contacts with the family after a tour. These seven "touches" take place within a couple weeks after the tour, if the family does not enroll.

Annette Gentry

We are grateful to Annette and her team for openly sharing the specifics of their follow-up campaign. In Annette's own words:

> *"At Creative Day School, we have learned the value of enrollment tracking and metrics. We use our own enrollment tracking form that is a slightly modified version of Kris's form. During management trainings, we emphasize the importance of obtaining all the information on the tracking form during the initial phone call. At Creative Day School, we also use a personalized version of Kris's phone script. We practice the script during role play sessions about once a month.*

> *"We have greatly increased our conversion ratio from calls to tours by using the script. We know how important it is to realize that this whole process takes time to implement and time to fine tune. We are always working on tweaking the process as we move along and learn what works for each of our center management. The key is to keep following-up with the family, no matter which type of contact you use, just keep at it until they either say "yes" or say "leave me alone" (which they rarely do).*

Follow-Up Step #1: Within a few days after the tour, center management sends a "Thank you for touring" card with a handwritten note inside. The card also has a slot for the management's business card. We had these cards printed with our name and logo on the front and the "thank you for touring" message inside with room for the personal, handwritten note.

Follow-Up Step #2: A phone call to the family within a week of the tour to follow-up and check in to see if an enrollment decision has been made. Often it is hard to catch parents during the day, so management do leave a message for the parent and about 50% of the time the parent will return the call.

Follow-Up Step #3: An email is sent to the parent with a special note about the tour and how much we are looking forward to the family joining our "Creative Day School" family. Often center management will attach to the email our center newsletter, a flyer with a coupon or an invitation to a special event at the center

Follow-Up Step #4: The next follow-up is another Kris Murray tip where we send a "special delivery" package addressed to the child with a gift for the child. When we mail this package, we usually include a book for the child and a note for the parent. The note can be a handwritten card or a letter to the parent placed inside the book cover. We make sure to put a label or a stamp inside the front cover that has our name, logo and contact information on it to continue to market our center to the parent as they read the book to the child.

Follow-Up Step #5: Another follow-up phone call is made to the family to check-in and see if a decision has been made. Often we will leave a message about how we are having a great day at Creative Day School and would love to have their child join us tomorrow. We may mention the teacher's name and some activity that is going on or the theme of the week.

Follow-Up Step #6: Another "snail mail" event as we have found that parents do respond positively to personalized mail. We will usually send out a pretty card with handwritten note inside, again mentioning something about the child, the tour or an event at the center. This time we include a free day card that offers one free day of child care for the potential enrollment.

Follow-Up Step #7: This step again depends on what our notes from the enrollment tracker tell us about how we best communicate with this family. Whatever the method we have found reaches the family and receives a response is how we will follow-up again with this family. If we have not been successful in reaching the family, we will typically email them with a request for a response if they are still interested, indicating that we are close to capacity in that classroom and slots are filling quickly.

As you can see, we do alternate the type of contact format as we go through the follow-up process. When you find which contact the parent prefers, do try to use that more frequently as you will get better responses. It is always better to personalize any notes or emails with names and whenever possible, throw in a detail you remember from the tour. Or you can also address a concern that came up during the tour by countering that concern with one of your center's unique benefits.

One other important point to mention, is that we use Kris's prospective parent questionnaire at the beginning of the tour. We have the parent come into the office or lounge to sit down and talk about their child care needs. We have the parent questionnaire on a clipboard and will either have the parent complete it on their own (only if the management needs a few minutes to prepare for the tour) or the center management will ask the parent the questions as if they were interviewing the parent to determine their child care needs and preferences. This questionnaire is vital to the success of the tour as it will guide you to the unique benefits that you need to emphasize and to the parent's concerns you will need to counter.

An important note here is that we have found that it often takes more than seven touches to reach a family and successfully convert them to an enrolled family. We have often had the family come to us 6 months after their initial contact with us. We keep the enrollment tracker on file for at least 6 months to a year, depending on the tracking results and continue to follow-up with the family.

After the first seven or more follow-ups, the prospects continue to receive at least our monthly newsletter attached to an email from Creative Day School, every month like clockwork."

Creative Day Schools' substantial increase in children (100 more enrolled) since they've started spending more time on follow-up is proof in the pudding that this strategy works.

Resource Link: For more information on Creative Day School, visit www.creativedayschool.net

Idea #42
Have an Email "Drip Campaign"

What's a "drip campaign?" Also known as an autoresponder series, it's a series of emails written in advance that automatically follow up with someone. The emails are pasted into your email management system or customer relationship management (CRM) system and you can set them up to send automatically on certain intervals, such as Day 1, Day 4, Day 8, etc. after a certain milestone or event.

For example, you might have a drip campaign for people after they tour. This would be part of your follow-up system as discussed on the prior page. You could have a similar but separate campaign for people who have not yet toured, providing them with enough information and incentives to come visit your school.

Often, drip campaigns are tied to the opt-in for your free report or "lead magnet". Someone opts in to get your freebie, say a child care checklist, then they start receiving informative and fun emails from you, to let them slowly get to know you.

Idea #43
Track Your Enrollment Funnel

An *enrollment funnel* is simply the process you undertake to market and promote your center to generate leads and convert them into customers.

Leads (also referred to as prospects or inquiries) are prospective customers who contact you for more information, take a tour of your facility, and eventually enroll in your program. *Enrollment funnel metrics* measure the results of each step in your marketing process that leads to an enrollment in order to determine its effectiveness.

When you are aware of your business's enrollment cycles throughout the year, you can prepare for them by timing your marketing efforts— and budget—appropriately. If, for example, you always have a high volume of leads in August, as many child care centers do, you and your staff can be better prepared for the increased number of phone call inquiries, e-mail inquiries, and, ideally, tours. On the flip side, you may want to plan your marketing expenditures for the times of the year that are traditionally more quiet.

Information about year-over-year trends in your business is extremely valuable for understanding the dynamics of your market's economy as well as supply versus demand. When you are aware of your business's year-over-year enrollment trends (comparing data from January 2014 to data from January 2013, for example), you will be better able to plan appropriately for peaks and valleys, marketing expenditures, and staff scheduling.

In addition to tracking and counting your raw number of leads, you need a reliable system for collecting key information about each prospect that contacts you. This information is extremely valuable because it allows you to follow up effectively with your prospects over time, and the process of gathering the information is an opportunity to build rapport and trust with the parent who is seeking child care. One of the biggest mistakes you can make is to work hard getting your phone to ring with new prospects, but then not have a system in place to ensure you and your staff are collecting as much information as possible about each prospect. If you're relying on a system of scraps of paper and sticky notes to gather prospect information, then you're leaving money on the table!

Community Marketing

Idea #44
Partner with Local Realtors

Remember the idea of marketing to families just moving in to the area? One of the best ways to do that is to partner with one or two of your favorite local realtors.

If you don't know any realtors, look for ones that are the "top producers" in your best neighborhoods. Simply drive around those neighborhoods and make a note of the agents with the most listings, based on for sale signs. You can also make connections with realtors and other business professionals through memberships in local groups like the Chamber of Commerce or Rotary Club.

The next step is to create some type of program and/or promotion that will appeal to realtors and their clients. Seek to make it a win-win-win for realtors, families, and you. For example, offer a "Free Child Care During Closing" coupon, or "Get to Know Us: Child Care on Moving Day for Just $10 Per Family". Moving is a stressful time, so if you can make it easier for families, you will build goodwill and great word of mouth in the community, not to mention new enrolling clients.

Idea #45
Do Weekly "Muffin Runs"

This is one of best strategies I know to get great word of mouth and increased "buzz" in your community. Everybody loves to get free food – it's that simple. Imagine your surprise and happiness if you worked at a local retail shop, salon, or office and someone came in with a huge basket full of yummy treats – muffins, bagels, cookies, donuts, whatever. You would probably remember the name of the business they were representing, wouldn't you?

What if they came not just once but every 4 or 5 weeks like clockwork? Would you be more likely to recommend them to others? (Of course!)

This is the beauty of the "muffin run" concept. Simply take some treats (either store-bought or baked by the kids in your school) to any local business that has the potential to send you business. Be sure to include plenty of brochures, testimonial flyers, and any promotions you are running. Target 4 or 5 businesses each week, maybe every Friday morning. What a great way to start the weekend – with smiles and community goodwill!

Here are some types of businesses you can put on your list. Any business that you do not compete with that attracts your ideal customer should be near the top:

Pediatricians	Pediatric dentists
OB/GYNs	Restaurants
Health & fitness clubs	Massage / spa
Women's and children's clothing shops	Managers of apartment complexes
Toy stores	Elementary schools
Salons, especially children's hair salons	
Realtors offices	

Idea #46
Participate in Parades

Everyone loves parades, but especially families with young children. Your program can participate in most if not all local parades, including large ones in nearby cities that may be "feeder towns" for you.

When you participate in a local parade, you should create a fun theme idea that can help you stand out. Match the theme to your brand, the parade theme (if any), or the time of year. Get matching t-shirts with your logo and maybe a cute saying on the back like "Ask Me Why I Love ABC Learning Center." Ask your current families and kids to march with you.

Finally, be sure to give away a cute promotional item with your logo on it. You could even give away bottles of water with a ribbon tied around the bottle attached to a small brochure or info card about your program. Maybe it could say "KEEP THIS CARD - $500 VALUE" and then provide a special offer for 2 weeks free tuition, when the cardholder enrolls by July 31.

Don't forget that for this and every photo opportunity you should snap a cute photo (or several) and post them on your Facebook page.

Get creative and have fun!

Idea #47
Host a Booth at Local Events

Community event participation can be a great way to keep your word of mouth elevated and positive. Local events can come in many flavors: family fun festivals, wine-tasting or musical events, holiday bazaars, "taste of" events, and Chamber of Commerce local business events just to name a few.

When you participate, you want to stand out and make your booth a really fun place for families and children. Ways to do this include:

- Have fun games with prizes for the little ones

- Have a drawing for a high-value early learning prize, such as a large Little Tykes playset or climber or a Leapster game console (I always recommend some sort of drawing so you can collect prospect information and mail them a follow-up, and/or call them)

- Have drawings for multiple "door prizes" that are announced on the half hour and draw people back to your booth to see if they won

- Have an interactive play-based feature like a sensory table, and change up what's in the table each half hour

- Have face-painting or temporary tattoos at your booth

- Provide healthy snacks and drinks

You also want your booth to match the venue and audience as much as possible. For example, you may decide you want to participate in the Chamber of Commerce event because you have a goal of building your professional network especially with dentists, pediatricians, and realtors. Therefore your booth might include materials about "how our businesses can help each other grow" and an iPad giveaway in exchange for business cards. This would be much different than what you'd offer at a family carnival.

Idea #48

Partner with Local Family Restaurants (Kids Eat Free)

As you probably know, many local family restaurants offer "Kids Eat Free" nights to bring in business, typically on slower nights of the week. You can boost your enrollment and get great word of mouth simply by adding fun value to the Kids Eat Free experience.

Simply decide who on your staff would like to earn extra money by providing fun and special childrens' experiences in the evening. Which teachers on your staff might excel at this? Just pull together some simple crafts, games, puzzles, and little goody bags with bubbles and trinkets from the dollar store, and you're all set. Be sure to put your brand on as many items as you can, and put your brochures and special offers in the goody bags. Ask the restaurant owner if you can provide printables with your logo and crayons to the kids.

Throw in a helium balloon for each child as they walk out the door, and you will be amazed at the reaction!

Again, to get started, just research which restaurants in your area offer Kids Eat Free nights and make a point to walk in repeatedly until you get to speak to the owner or manager. Have your idea in place and make sure you tell him you're going to promote it with YOUR families so you'll also be sending him some new customers. Make it a win-win where you seek to add value to their customer experience.

Idea #49
Find Reciprocal Referral Partners

One of the best ways to expand your influence and word of mouth is to have a Reciprocal Referral program. This encompasses many of the professionals and businesses we've already mentioned – people who are doing business with your ideal customers, but with whom you do not compete.

Your first step is to make a list of any and all businesses in your draw area who attract and cater to families with young children. Then you want to create the "meat" of your Reciprocal Referral program. It could be as simple as a verbal agreement or "handshake" that you and your partner will cross-promote one another to gain new prospects and hopefully customers or clients. This is typically supported with brochures and promotional materials in eachother's establishments. You could opt to take it one step further, and offer your partners a special "partner-only" promotional rate or free-week offer.

On letterhead, type up a brief summary of your new Referral Partner program and clearly state what's "in it for them". For example, "we'd like to place your materials in our lobby so your business can gain new customer from our loyal families in exchange for you doing the same."

You can take this idea one step further by providing access to your customers for services that fit your program. For example, you probably already have a local pediatric dentist come into your program and teach kids about dental health. Likewise, you may offer portraits and children's haircuts. I've even seen centers that offer parents a dry-cleaning service and prepared dinners. These are natural opportunities for you to extend a partnership and to develop some sort of cross-promotional program with these businesses.

Idea #50
Corporate Discounts / Preferred Employer Programs

This one idea can dramatically fill up your program, but like anything with a potentially huge payoff, it takes time and effort. The concept is to put your child care program on the employee benefit list for mid-size to large local employers. Obviously, this is not going to work with employers who offer in-house child care – unless they're always full and cannot accommodate all their employees who need it. Then you could become their top "overflow" choice and these employees will be calling you.

So what are the steps to accomplishing this? First, you need to create a special program just for your "preferred employer clients". They need to feel special and that their employees are receiving something that's not available to the general public. It could be a 5-7% tuition discount across the board. It could be these employees are not charged your annual re-registration fee and they get two weeks free each year (a $525 value). It's up to you and what your market wants in order to make it worth their while.

Once you create your program and get some materials created (a brochure plus a glossy flyer should do it) you can approach every company in your area and start getting the word out. It helps to have a current database of where all your parents currently work, so you can target those companies you are already drawing from. If you can say "we have three of your employees already using us and here are testimonials from them about how much they love us" it will help you get in the door to a much greater degree. Your level of professionalism and the value you bring the company are harbingers of your success with this strategy. Good luck!

Idea #50: Preferred Employer Program / Corporate Discounts

CASE STUDY:

Tina Kitchens, HoneyTree Learning Centers

Beth and Tina of HoneyTree

HoneyTree Learning Centers offer a high-quality child care experience in and around Roanoke, Virginia.

Executive Director Tina Kitchens has worked for HoneyTree for 28 years so she's seen the company grow and change in many ways over the years. One of the ways the program really has consistently grown is through partnerships with local businesses and employers.

HoneyTree has special "preferred employer" relationships with several large companies in the area, including two hospitals and a large law firm. The incentives that make these relationships a win-win include a discount program for employees. Discounts range from 10% - 15% off regular tuition to a subsidy program in which the employer pays for a portion of the tuition.

HoneyTree promotes these special programs at employee benefit "fairs", attending new hire orientations and by putting their brochures inside the businesses and their new hire packets. These programs help bring HoneyTree a consistent flow of new leads from families in the area.

Resource Link:
Learn more about HoneyTree Learning Centers at www.HoneyTreeELC.com.

Idea #51
Press Releases

You may not realize it, but there are many press-worthy happenings and events that take place in your program. People love any news stories that have to do with children, especially the adorable little ones in your center or school. Moreover, many print media and online media are constantly looking for new story ideas to add human interest to their publication. That's where you can help.

A press release is simply a one-page document that informs local media about a newsworthy event, story, or situation. Anyone can write and submit one. You can see examples of real press releases at PRWeb. com, that you can model.

So what should you write about? Let's start with local events. We've discussed several types in this book. Use a press release to alert the local media that you're hosting a family-friendly event that's open to the public. Another great topic is community contributions. If you do a toy drive or coat drive at holiday time, or you do a Hop-a-Thon for Muscular Dystrophy, write a press release about how much food you collected or how many total "hops" your kids did to help Jerry's kids.

Set a goal to submit one press release per quarter, or create a marketing calendar and plan out which events you're going to focus on this year. That way you'll be sure to get it done and not let it slip through the cracks. The media editors will appreciate the fact that you took the time to provide them with content. Your release may not always get "picked up" but don't give up. Persistence and consistency is key with this idea.

Idea #52
Develop Relationships with Pediatricians and OB-GYNs

On your enrollment paperwork for a new child, do you ask the name of the child's pediatrician? If they are 3 years or more in age, do you ask who their pediatric dentist is? I'll bet you do. If not, you need to start, if only to know who to call in a medical (or dental) emergency in case the parents can't be reached.

Now that you have that information for each child, create a list or database of doctors your clients are seeing. This is a powerful list. It's a way for you to determine who the top 3 or 4 physicians (and top 1 or 2 dentists) your clients are using. You can then contact these doctors and use this information to "open the door" to building a relationship with them.

The conversation would go something like this: "Hi Doctor Smith, this is Kris and I'm the owner of ABC Learning Academy. I've noticed that over 50% of my clientele use you as their child's pediatrician. I just wanted to call and connect with you, and I want to make sure we are doing everything possible to promote the health and wellness of the kids in your care, since you're the expert."

See how I appealed to the ego of the doctor? Do you think this approach could work for you? When you build a positive relationship with these pediatricians and dentists (accompanied by gifts of muffins and bagels for their staff as discussed on Page 61) you will naturally start getting extremely valuable referrals from these authority figures in your community.

(I hope you are excited about this idea because it's one of the best, most powerful ones in this book!)

Idea #53
Host Public-Welcome Events at Your School

Your facility is likely a very positive and fun place for children and families, and it's probably being underutilized as an asset. It's a good idea to have prospective families (as well as current customers) get in the habit of coming to your location for high-value activities that set you apart as the local expert in early learning (which you are!).

There are generally three categories of events to which you can invite the public at large:

- Parent Seminars: Host speakers or topics related to parenting or family issues. You as the owner or director (and resident expert) can speak on a topic that's important to you, something you specialize in.

  Seminars on sleep issues, challenging behavior, and potty-training tips can be very popular.

- Parents Nights Out: Provide a 3-hour evening of low-cost care for parents both in your center and for new parents & children, if your state allows it. Be sure to have them fill out a form with all their information so you can follow up with them.

- Presentations for Kids: Animal shows, the Bubble Lady, magicians, musical guests, etc.

Make a big splash with these events, including ads, flyers, a page on your website, invitations to everyone on your list, signage, and as many other affordable ways you can think of to get the word out. Test different times and days of the week to see what brings the best crowd. Offer current parents to "bring a friend" and both will receive a small gift.

Idea #54
Host a Family Carnival

Similar to the previous idea, the Family Carnival or "Fun-Fest" brings both existing customers and new prospects to your facility. I like the idea of doing this as a Customer Appreciation Event and also as a new twist on the Open House. As a trend, open houses have been losing interest over the past few years so you'll do better if you re-label it something fun and fresh, and communicate the new fun activities that are going to take place.

Here are some ideas for what to feature at your Carnival to make it buzz with excitement:

- Have it outside on the grounds of your school, especially if you can fairly reliably expect good weather and you have nice grounds
- Bring in a huge Bounce House (be sure to have it monitored with a limit of kids and age groups)
- Face-painting
- Arts and crafts
- Games and sensory tables
- Obstacle course
- Scavenger hunt on-site for the kids or as a family
- Photo booth
- Massage stations for parents
- Food / barbeque
- Clowns, magicians, animal shows, or other performers
- Bubble machine
- Children's musical performers or stage acts
- Balloon animal guy/gal
- What else can you think of? ;-)

As always, BE SURE to collect names and addresses of every attending family, and make a note if they were told (referred) about the carnival by an existing family. Ask current families to "bring a friend". Have fun!

Idea #55
Advertise in Apartment Complexes

You may draw a sizable segment of your customers from apartment complexes or townhome developments. You can befriend the managers of these facilities with a basket of treats, then ask permission to blanket the complex with brochures, flyers, and promotional offers.

It's smart to customize your marketing message to <u>speak as personally and directly to your prospect as possible.</u> Maybe you create a special letter with the headline:

**"Several of Our Current Families Are Your Neighbors.
We Welcome All 'Rolling Hills' Children with Open Arms!"**

or

**"All 'Rolling Hills' Families Save $500 on Tuition
when Enrolled by May 31!"**

Apartment complexes usually have centralized mailboxes in the lobby, so it's fairly easy to reach the residents in one fell swoop, especially if the manager lets you put a letter in each of the boxes.

In townhome developments, you can ask for permission to advertise in the clubhouse or other centrally visited areas within the complex.

Strengthen Customer Relationships

Idea #56:
Digital Parent Communication System

There's an emerging trend in how teachers and directors communicate throughout the day with parents, and you're likely aware of it. Technology is now allowing teachers and parents to communicate electronically using digital "parent-teacher communication tools". These are software solutions that are typically hosted online or "in the cloud." Programs who've adopted them are benefitting in a variety of ways.

First and foremost, parents are able to have increased peace of mind due to the connection they have with their child. In many programs, teachers have been trained to capture 3, 5, even 10 photos of each child in their classroom and individually transmit these digital photos

RESOURCES

I recommend and endorse three of these systems, primarily due to the fact they are all "blessed" by my clients. All have different strengths and features.

Tadpoles: Learn more at www.tadpoles.com

KidReports: Learn more at www.kidreports.com

LifeCubby: Learn more at www.LifeCubby.me

to the parents (and even to grandparents) throughout the day, every day.

For parents of infants and toddlers, in particular, these photos mean everything. Now the parent is connected to the child and feels more a part of his or her day. If the child is not good about sharing his/her day, the photos (and electronic daily sheet) allow the parent to engage with the child at the end of the day through pictures.

Finally, these systems eliminate the daily paper sheets given to parents about the child's day, which obviously is a greener solution than wasting all that paper. Plus, the systems are archived so both teachers and parents have a full record of development over time. Teachers love using these systems for the most part, and it's great for supporting your licensing or accreditation regarding child history.

Idea #57:
Referral Rewards Program

You could probably fill up your program just by having an effective referral rewards program. The problem is, most child care leaders don't communicate it well, or they give too small of a reward, so it's not memorable and it doesn't motivate people to take time to refer.

What is a customer really worth to you? This should help put the size of your referral reward into context. On average, a client family is worth $25,000 in revenue on average, based on child care programs I work with, and more if they have multiple children. So how much are you willing to reward people if they send you a new client? I generally advise that your reward should be $100 at minimum, and up to $500 or more. You want your referral program to generate excitement, right?

I get asked this question all the time: is it better to give cash or a break on tuition, as the reward? It depends. When offered the choice, parents often take the free tuition because the overall dollar value can be higher. However, the KEY to increasing your referrals is to demonstrate the joy and excitement that parents are getting when they refer, and telling that story.

The best way to demonstrate this is to snap a photo or quick video of the moment you hand them the reward. Just have your iPhone or iPad handy when you hand them the $100 dollar bill, or the Gift Certificate for a parents night out with dinner, limo, wine, and child care included! Their excitement captured in a photo and then posted on your social media pages (especially Facebook) AND in your parent newsletter can really drive up the momentum of your program.

Idea #57: Referral Rewards Program

CASE STUDY:

Aleta Mechtel,
Children of Tomorrow

Aleta Mechtel is the owner of two child care centers outside of Minneapolis. When I started working with Aleta back in 2010, she had built a high-quality program with amazing teacher and family relationships. She had worked hard to create a wonderful experience for her community, but she wasn't leveraging it because she had no structured Referral Rewards program. Here is her story in her own words:

> *"My first year starting my monthly referral rewards program, our families referred 13 new families to our school. Some with multiple children! I made it a priority to build strong relationships with the surrounding businesses that my family base used and created my reward from their product. They advertised for me, as I did for them.*
>
> *"I wanted to do an end of the year referral drawing that did not make me go broke! I partnered with the local travel agency and told them what I was doing. They offered to match whatever I was willing to put in for my drawing. Keep in mind you need to let the partner know just how much advertising they would get out of this!*
>
> *"I decided to hold my drawing live and on stage at our holiday performance. At the entrance of the theater, our staff were handing out programs that were stuffed with the travel agency's brochure. We not only had parents attend, but grandparents, aunt and uncles and some friends of*

the family got that advertisement! I went up on stage, introduced myself, thanked them for coming and proceeded to let them know how important they all were in success of COT...with that being said let them know that I had one other surprise. All 13 families who had referred throughout the year were put into a drawing, right there on stage, for a $500.00 travel voucher for our lucky winner! I only had to pay $250 and the travel agency got to advertise to a lot of people all at once! (A win-win-win!)"

"Always remember your graduated families! Keep in touch with them, send them notes of hello-stay on their radar! They too can be a referral base for you and make sure to send all graduated families a $100-$150 Visa card for spreading the good word of your center! One more idea - we change our reward each month to match the seasonal time of year and to keep it fresh."

Aleta is now getting 15 to 25 referrals per year for each of her schools, which helps keep her full. Way to go!

Resource Link: Learn more about Aleta and Children of Tomorrow at www.childrenoftomorrow.com

Idea #58:
Referral Cards for Staff

Staff and teachers want to get in the action too! Arm your teachers with personalized business cards, and maybe make this a "perk" for staying with your program for at least 90 days. On the back of the card, print a statement that says the following:

FUN FAMILIES AND TEACHERS WANTED!

Whether you are a potential client or employee, we want to meet you! Please bring this card into our school and the staff person whose name is on the front will receive a cash reward of $100 or more! Thank you and we can't wait to meet you!"

If you see that your staff are not motivated and excited to tell others in the community about you, you know you have a morale and culture problem. It's time to look in the mirror and figure out why your teachers are not excited to be your employees.

Idea #59:
Birthday Signs or "Student of the Month" Signs in Yards

Want to make every child in your program feel extra-special? This strategy does just that, while providing great exposure for your brand and the name of your program. The idea is to get some changeable yard signs that say "Student of the Month" or "Happy Birthday" with a place to insert or customize the sign with the child's name, and then you put the sign in his/her yard.

CASE STUDY:
Thad Joiner, Sunbrook Academy

Sunbrook Academy is a multi-unit child care franchise operating throughout Georgia. Owner Thad Joiner and his talented team at Sunbrook are consistently looking for new and creative ways to attract and retain customers. Thad purchased Sunbrook Academy after five years of revenue

Student of the Month Sign

decreases - in year one of ownership he and his team have created an increase of over 50 percent in revenue at multiple units. Wow!

One of the creative ways they market Sunbrook Academy is their Student of the Month program. Each month a student from each classroom is a winner. They receive recognition in the email Newsletter, outside their classrooms, and most importantly with their very own Star Sign to go in their front yard at home. These signs are noticed by everyone who drives by their house, and makes for a great memory for each of the students that are awarded.

If a center wants a program that increases enrollment by addressing both attraction and retention, this is an easy program to get off the ground.

Resource Link: Learn more about Sunbrook Academy at www.sunbrookacademy.com

Idea #60:
Birthday Cards Mailed Home

Anyone can hand a birthday card to a child, but it takes a little extra effort and attention to mail a card to the child's home. You can semi-automate this by tracking everyone's birthdays by week, and the week before have cards on hand for all the teachers to sign. Mail them all out on Saturday and you're good to go.

Or you can fully automate this idea by using a system like SendOut-Cards (see page 26 for more details). Simply enter all your children's names, addresses, and birth dates into the system and the cards will be mailed in advance, personalized and all.

Idea #61:
Birthday Cards for Parents

I'm not sure I know of a more heart-warming and thoughtful gesture than saying "Happy Birthday" to mom or dad from their child. When you facilitate this, you will certainly be seen as the "hero" of the day, and your word of mouth will soar. You can do this a couple ways – if you have a digital photo-sharing system like Tadpoles or KidReports, you can take a picture of the child holding a "Happy Birthday" sign, and email it to the parent.

You could have the child create a card or piece of artwork for mom or dad, and mail it home to the parent. Or you could have the child color a frame, and put a cute photo of the child inside the frame with a birthday message for the parent. There are so many creative ways to celebrate. And these are the special touches that your program will be remembered for, long after the child enters Kindergarten.

Idea #62:
Family "Connection" Events

"We are living in the connection economy".
~ SETH GODIN, AUTHOR

When families in your center or school feel like they are connected to one another, your retention and overall customer satisfaction will be higher. Of course, one way to do this is through social media using techniques like a private Facebook group to allow the parents to post chit-chat and photos.

I like the idea of having monthly "connection" events both inside and outside of your facility. Many of you celebrate various holidays in your school with parents and grandparents in attendance, and that's great. Consider taking it one step further and hosting events outside your school. Here are some ideas:

- Sledding party at the local sledding hill
- Ice-skating party at the local ice rink
- Picnic / barbeque at the town park, reserving the pavilion
- Family nature walks
- Zoo or museum trips for the whole family
- Pet parade with kids and their pets, either at the park or at your school
- Pizza party out on the town
- Chuck E Cheese's / play center party
- Mommy and me yoga on Saturdays

Idea #63:
Parent Newsletter

I believe that every small business, including child care centers, can benefit from a customer newsletter. Your newsletter is a fantastic way to build relationships with customers and prospects, so it's a great enrollment and retention tool. It has "pass-along" value so it can aid in building referrals with new clients.

The mistake I most often see in child care is that each classroom teacher will create his or her own "newsletter" but this is often times just a list of birthdays and a lunch/snack menu. It might include a brief blurb from the teacher of that classroom, or a curriculum update. This method of so-called Parent Newsletter has a low perceived value and falls short of the mark, in my opinion.

I recommend a center-wide newsletter with monthly columns that pique interest and gain a "following". One effective approach is to make mini-celebrities of your families, children, and teachers by featuring them in your newsletter. Monthly columns could feature fun human-interest stories like "Teacher Q&A" (where you get to know the personal interests and life of a teacher); "Ask the Expert: Director Sally's Parenting Tip of the Month"; "Monthly Rembrandt: (Featuring a Child and His/Her Artwork)"; and you could also have a "Thanks for Your Referrals" column, listing the names of everyone who has referred that month, along with a photo of them receiving the referral reward (perhaps an oversized cardboard $100 bill).

These types of columns, interspersed with the regular fare of menus, curriculum themes, puzzles, and events, will increase your newsletter readership.

I also recommend printing your newsletter out and mailing it home to your families. This will get the thing read more, adds a special touch, and increase its perceived value even more. When it's distributed via email or in the cubbies, your newsletter will more often get deleted or end up on the floor of the car. And after your hard work, you want your newsletter to work for you.

Develop Your Value Platform

Idea #64:
Video Testimonials

I'm really glad that you're still reading this book, because buried here as Idea #64 is probably the number one strategy in this entire book.

Video testimonials. The number one fastest and most credible way to build trust with parents – both online and offline. Online, you can use them on almost every digital media and social networking platform, or at least link to them from your social media sites. Offline, you can pull them together onto a DVD that you mail out to prospects, or have them on a reel that you show to people during the tour. Video testimonials are the "proof in the pudding" that will sell your center online before a prospect ever comes to take a tour.

So it's incredible to me that so many of you STILL do not have them on your website. Heck, many of you don't even have written ones! This is a huge mistake for your enrollment and the health of your business.

To get started, you just need a basic videocamera, including the one that comes with your phone or tablet. Simply ask a parent who loves you to please provide a quick 60-second testimonial. Provide them with a few "starter questions" so they have a guide as to what you want them to speak about. Things like "what were you looking for in a preschool", "why did you choose us", "how have we helped your child", and "who would you recommend us to" will be very powerful for other parents to see and hear.

Idea #64: Video Testimonials on Your Website

CASE STUDY:
Chris Flaxbeard,
Premier Academy

Chris Flaxbeard is the owner of two child care locations in Omaha, Nebraska. Chris is a strong marketer who does a lot to keep her schools fully enrolled. Her website includes both written and video testimonials.

Chris Flaxbeard

The videos are very powerful, and they follow the simple format of the questions provided on the prior page, which gives parents an easy guide to making a great video for you.

Chris and her staff follow these steps to obtain great parent video testimonials:

1) We ask parents to videotape a testimonial at our "event parties" (i.e. Halloween Party or Christmas Party) because they are usually "glowing" with happiness and enthusiasm with the event and saying such great, positive things!

2) We provide a "cue" card with points for them to discuss:
   • First Name
   • First Name and Age of Child
   • What they like best about Premier Academy!

3) We then make simple edits if needed and post the videos to our website and to our YouTube channel.

Another good time we found to ask for testimonials is when a parent would come up to the director or asst. director and tell her all of the great things they just witnessed, realized, etc. The key is to have a video-camera ready at all times! We use a smart phone. The moms would want to "come back" another day more dressed up or with make-up on. But the less professional the video looks and the more it looks like real-life families the more the video is trusted by people visiting your website.

Resource Link: Learn more about Chris and Premier Academy by visiting www.PremierAcademyInc.com. Watch their parent video testimonials at www.premieracademyinc.com/testimonials

Idea #65
Written Testimonials Everywhere

Simply put, you cannot have too many parent testimonials in your marketing. They are worth their weight in gold. Why? Because they build trust for your program. What others say about you has been shown to be about 20 times more credible than what you say about yourself.

So I recommend making a list of all the effective and sometimes unusual places you can put your written testimonials. Here is a partial list. Pick 5 of these and get started:

- On your signage / banners
- On your hold music
- On your website
- On your social media sites
- Framed on the walls of your center
- Framed in the bathroom of your center
- In your Parent Newsletter
- On your van
- At the bottom of your email signature
- In email blasts to prospects
- In your e-Packet (see Idea #29)

Don't stop with parent testimonials – teachers want to get in the act, too. When you put teacher testimonials on your website and in social media, you'll generate more qualified teacher leads and you'll be more likely to have a hiring back-up plan in case you have unexpected turnover.

Idea #66:
Hold a Testimonial Contest

Maybe you're inspired by the idea of using testimonials but you have one big problem. You don't have any. One easy way to get a handful or two of great testimonials is to have a contest.

Here's how it works. You can use a survey system like SurveyMonkey and email the details of your contest to your parent list, you can do the contest through regular email, or you can do it with paper either mailed home or in cubbies. However you choose to communicate it, here's what your contest should contain:

1) A deadline. Give your parents a 7 to 10 day window to enter the contest.

2) The rules. "Everyone who submits a testimonial that follows these guidelines will be entered into a random drawing for a (insert something of value).

3) Questions or Thought-starters for what you're looking for. You'll get better "juicier" testimonials if you ask for things like "why did you choose us", "what do you love most about us", "how have we helped your child", etc. Ideally parents will rave about what makes you special and how you've helped their child succeed.

4) A Prize. It could be a free week of tuition, an iPad or device, cash, a Romance Package, free gas or groceries, you name it. It should have a real value of at least $100, preferably closer to $250 or more.

5) An effective way to communicate the contest.

6) A reminder right before the deadline.

You should get at least 10% of parents to participate, especially if you do one or two reminders a day or two before the deadline. If you have 60 familes enrolled, that's 6 great testimonials. Excellent start!

Idea #67:
Find Your "Hook"

The idea of setting yourself apart from other child care and preschool programs in your market is massively important. It's so important, that we've dedicated Ideas 67, 68 and 69 in this book to this strategy. The problem is, most owners and leaders don't take the time to figure out their unique value, let alone communicate it effectively and consistently.

Let's start with your hook. A "hook" is also sometimes referred to as a "Unique Selling Proposition" or "Unique Value Statement". It's the umbrella under which you answer the question "how am I different than any other child care program in town?"

It might be easiest to demonstrate a hook by giving you some examples. These are all real-world examples of hooks that program owners created to set themselves apart:

- "The only program in central Ohio focused on health and wellness for children."

- "The only program with a Formal Kindergarten Readiness program."

- "The longest-running program in the area, established in 1967. More years of experience than any other."

- "The only program with a 30-day Happy Family satisfaction guarantee."

- "The only program focused on the arts for children, offering piano, guitar, dance, multi-media arts, and much more."

How can you find your hook? Focus in on your passion – is it sports, nature, wellness, organics, arts? Or do a competitive analysis and spend time really discovering how you are different. You may need to "create" your hook by adding new unique value.

Idea #68
Identify Your Unique Benefits

Hand in hand with finding your value platform "hook", is the process of getting clear about how you uniquely benefit your customers, that is, children and parents. Your goal is to be able to communicate a list of 5 to 10 unique benefits that are tangible, easy to comprehend, and meaningful to parents.

For example, often when I ask leaders to do this exercise, they come up with things like "quality of care" or "our curriculum". This is not what we're after, because while they may be unique, they are not tangible and it's not readily apparent to parents what they mean. (Stay away from "industry-speak" terms like DAP at all costs because parents eyes start glazing over).

Ideally, your unique benefits and features list would also focus on things that truly differentiate you from your competitors. You can get a handle on this by doing some competitive analysis. List your top 5 competitors and visit their websites, request information from their websites (if offered), even call them pretending to be a parent, and consider sending in a friend or colleague to "mystery shop" them. The more you are clear about what they offer, the easier it is to develop how you're unique and special – even if it means you'll need to add some competitive differentiators to your program.

Use the list of unique benefit ideas on the following page to help you get started. Another fantastic process is to create a little questionnaire and hand it out to every employee in the company, asking for their input on this. Then compile the results and use this input to develop your unique benefit list.

Unique Benefits and Features for Your Program:
Use this List to Get Started

Which of these do you currently offer, that set you apart in your market? Which can you *add* as new differentiating value, and/or competitive advantage?

- Free diapers
- Largest playground
- Indoor playground
- Fresh fruit & veggies
- Organic meals
- Transportation
- Accreditations
- Special programs (baby yoga)
- "Best of" award
- ZONO (cleaner, no bleach)
- State of the art security
- Online camera system
- Teacher tenure / degrees
- On-site owner
- Longest in market
- Multiple generations attended
- Owned by a local mom
- Homework Club
- Activities all-inclusive
- Paperless daily sheets
- Daily photos / videos sent electronically
- Eco-Healthy certified

Idea #68: Identify Your Unique Benefits

CASE STUDY:

Rochelle Kiner,
The Oxford School

Rochelle Kiner is the owner of two child care locations in the Columbus, Ohio area. Rochelle understands the importance of setting her schools apart from other child care and preschool programs in her market, especially because she competes with several high-end chains and franchises. Here is her story:

Rochelle Kiner

"We set about to identify our program's unique-ness by touring a number of childcare centers and hearing what's said over and over – much of which is just industry speak that the average parents don't really understand. Then we sat down as an administrative team and created a list of features and things we're exceptionally good at. From there we still weren't 100% clear on what makes us unique and how to make it different from all the others we'd heard during tours. Next we broke that list down into groups of items that were similar or within the same overall category. As those categories were created it became clear how we're unique and definitely stand out from our competitors.

"Here is how we now communicateour unique benefits to prospects and customers, both on the tour and in marketing materials:

- *We're the only childcare and preschool program in central Ohio focused on health and wellness.*

- *We're not a chain, we're privately owned and operated by a local couple with children in the program.*

- *We provide our families updates and pictures throughout your child's day so you always know what's going on with your child.*

- *Plus, we have a happy family guarantee – so when you join our program if you decide we're not a good fit for your family for any reason we'll refund up to a month of tuition no questions asked.*

"Since defining our unique brilliance we've not only been able to better communicate with prospects, our staff have been able to better understand why we do what we do, keep our focus and messaging consistent and most importantly improve our programs to reflect what's truly most important to our mission."

Resource Link: See videos of Rochelle and her school, and learn more about The Oxford School by visiting www.TheOxfordSchool.com

Idea #69:
Communicate Your 3 Big Differences

Now that you have clarity on your unique benefits list, you will really set yourself apart if you can pick the 3 or 4 "best" or "biggest" differences between you and competitors, and be able to communicate them easily and succinctly to callers and visitors.

Ideally this would be part of your phone script:

> "Mary, may I share with you the 3 ways we are really different from any other child care program in the area?"

> "Sure."

> "Well, we have the largest indoor play space in the area, we serve organic meals, and we have a formal Kindergarten Readiness program."

> "Wow. Organic meals, that's really cool, I've been trying to serve organic dairy and meats at home."

> "Absolutely. Health and wellness are really important to the owners of the school, the Johnsons, so we've been serving 100% organic menus for over two years. Hopefully when you come visit the school you'll be able to meet the Johnsons, they are here a couple days a week."

Boom! You just made a connection with Mary that she's going to remember. This strategy is extremely powerful because it's actually more important for you to be different in your prospect's mind than it is to be "high-quality". Many programs these days are high-quality. But how many have spent the time figuring out how they are truly different and special?

Idea #70:
Tell Your Story

In the world of "main street" businesses, people don't actually buy from companies – they buy from people. Think about this: people do business with people they know, like and trust. These days, there are many ways you can build relationships with prospects and customers – both offline and online.

One of the very best ways (as well as one of the least-used ways) is to engage people by telling your personal story. Customers want to be connected to the owner and employees of companies they do business with, and that means that your business will grow if you share your personal story. You can tell many aspects of your story – often one that works really well is the "origin story". This is the story of why you decided to get into business as a child care owner. What motivated and inspired you to work in early childhood? What is your vision and what do you consider to be your "mission in life"?

Another personal story you can tell is your family background and your interests. Just a one-page story "from the owner" to your prospects, with the fact that this is a family-owned business and you run it with your wife, accompanied by a family photo, is enough to engage with people and set you apart in their minds as someone they could get to know, like, and trust. If you were a mom trying to choose a child care program, and you received a personal letter with a photo from the owners, wouldn't you be more likely to at least take a tour of that school – versus a corporate-run facility with no "get to know us" letter? Based on the results I've seen firsthand from owners who tell their story, I know the answer is a resounding "yes".

CASE STUDY:
Bob and Bettina Crenshaw, Brenwood Academy

People want to do business with people they know, like, and trust. In the world of child care, that's especially true. As a parent, I want to know that the owners of my child's learning center are actively involved and they are passionate about making the experience a high-quality, excellent one.

Bettina & Bob on their wedding day

Bob and Bettina Crenshaw had a great personal "story" but when I met them, they were not telling it. They took a leap of faith to put themselves in the "spotlight" when I reassured them that people really want to know them. It's kind of like being friends with the owner or chef at your favorite restaurant – you're going to dine there more often if you have that personal connection.

Bob and Bettina brought a professional video team to their school, to create multiple videos for their website. One of these was an introductory video of them as the owners – a "get acquainted" video. They also wrote a "Letter from the Owners" to allow prospects and customers to get to know them better. This letter is featured on the following pages.

Since implementing these "Tell Your Story" strategies and other best practices in this book, Bob and Bettina's enrollment has grown and they are opening a new private elementary program.

Resource Link: See Bob's videos and learn more about Brenwood Academy by visiting www.BrenwoodAcademy.com

Letter from the Owners: Bob & Bettina's Story

Bob and Bettina Crenshaw's story is a long one. Born just one day apart and together since the third grade, they were high school sweethearts living in Miami, Florida. Married while Bob was still in his senior year at the University of Florida, they moved back to Miami after he graduated to begin their careers and start their family.

Their first daughter born in 1980 marked the beginning of the Crenshaw's journey in child development and care. Bettina left her job in the corporate world to raise their first daughter, Nichole, but needing additional income it was quickly decided that Bettina would start her first family childcare business. Bob's job soon took the family to Chatsworth, California and a second daughter, Erica, was born. Bettina's home child development and care home (now with 18 children in the home) was just not enough.

The Crenshaws started their first mail-order preschool curriculum business where daily lesson plans and activity kits along with all the supplies were sold nationwide to other family child care providers, church based preschools, and small independent child care centers. With yet another job opportunity, now in Las Cruces, New Mexico, the family packed up again and relocated. With this move, Bettina carried on her family childcare business, and next came a boy, Ryan, to finish out the Crenshaw family.

Believe it or not, another job opportunity resulted in relocation to Fairfax, Virginia where the mail-order business was put to rest, and the family childcare business continued. The Crenshaw's were tired of moving. A major life and business decision was made to make one more move to the Atlanta area where the family had close ties and had just fallen in love with the life style and family oriented yet rural settings of Canton. While in Virginia, the Crenshaws constructed their first childcare center, then named The Kid Connection, in the Hickory Flat community with the desire to bring only the highest level of quality to the very rural setting. Many people thought a new church or bank was being built, as no childcare facility in the area looked anything like the specifically designed facility going up in their community. With the opening, the Crenshaws made their last move to Georgia.

Several years later, a second center was opened in the city of Holly Springs, followed by the third in Macedonia. The Crenshaws enjoyed twenty years of success with their three child development centers and are very proud to say that their little group of schools became the very first Preschool School System accredited by SACS (the Southern Association of Colleges and Schools) in the entire country. As the focus of the Macedonia center was changing to a more academic setting with desires to begin offering Kindergarten and elementary curriculum, this school was rebranded with the name Brenwood Academy. Other highlights include the fact that the schools were one of the first 10 selected in the state to begin the Georgia Lottery Funded Pre-Kindergarten Program in it's first year of trials. The schools were accredited by NAEYC, and the Crenshaws were both very active in the Georgia Child Care Association, Cherokee County CASA, Quality Assist, and with the Georgia Department of Education Early Childhood Division.

The Crenshaw family was struck by their biggest challenge in early 2011 when Bettina was diagnosed with cancer, and several other debilitating auto-immune diseases. This caused the family to take a very serious look at their personal life in relation to their business activities and the resulting very difficult decision was made – the two original centers were to be closed so the family could focus on Bettina's health and the concentration of the further development of Brenwood Academy.

Thankfully, Bettina's cancer is now in remission, but she still has daily issues with other medical conditions that keep her from her first love – dealing on a daily basis with the children at Brenwood Academy. Both Bob and Bettina are very active in the management and operations of the school with the help of a first class management team and a fantastic team of dedicated teachers and staff. Bob and Bettina are proud of the thousands of children that they have helped raise, educate, and care for over the last thirty three years and we look to continue with the children enrolled today and in the future at Brenwood Academy.

Idea #71:
Match Your Market

Every market has unique characteristics that make it special. Some markets are highly affluent, others are economically disadvantaged. Some markets are blue-collar (with a typically high need for 2nd shift care) and others are white-collar. College and university towns have their own special behaviors and demographics. It's up to you to understand the unique dynamics of your market.

Moreover, where you are located within your market is really important. What companies and employers are you near? Are you in a business or industrial area, closer to where people work - or more in a neighborhood, where customers live? This will also determine how you can and should market to potential customers. (Use the Map it Out strategy on Page 21 to gain clarity on this).

The point is, your value message and what you offer should be a match to your ideal customers within your market. For a college market, offer organic meals and get the "Green" certification from Eco Healthy Child Care. For a manufacturing area, offer 2nd shift care. For an affluent professional market, offer a Montessori blend or a focus on the arts. If it's a big sports-loving town, include sports and athletics in the curriculum. You get the idea.

If your location is suffering with layoffs and companies moving out of the area, you would be smart to set a long-term goal to sell your program and move to a growing area. Most child care owners don't like when I tell them this, and of course it's your choice to make. I'd personally rather do business in a thriving and growing market than one that is shrinking or low income.

Idea #72:
Add a ZONO

Many of you have not heard about the ZONO sanitation system, so I'm taking a page in this book to inform you about this revolutionary way to sanitize literally everything in your school that's not glued down. The ZONO (pictured below) was created by my buddy Walter Mann in his garage, in response to his teenagers' smelly gym gear and the growing concern over staph infections at school for athletes.

Today, many of my Child Care Success Academy members have a

> **RESOURCE**
>
> If you're interested in learning more about ZONO, please visit **www.zonosanitech.com.** When you mention **promo code "Kris101"** you'll be eligible for a special "bulk pricing" discount that's not available anywhere else.

ZONO in their schools. It's a massive competitive advantage for schools, because you can alleviate parents' fears about germs and illness. With a ZONO you can literally sanitize anything to a 99.9% germ-free level - stuffed animals, crayons, cots, blankets – as long as it fits inside the ZONO cabinet. There are single-door and double-door models to fit any space in your child care center.

Regulations vary by state regarding the approved use of the ZONO to meet sanitation requirements.

Two-door ZONO cabinet

Idea #73:
Use Holidays in Your Marketing

Everyone loves holidays! When you integrate holidays into your marketing message, it can break through the clutter and add a massive element of fun to your promotions and relationship-building. After all, you are likely already celebrating holidays inside the walls of your school (Dr. Seuss's birthday, Mother's Day, Valentine's Day, etc.) so why not extend the fun to your marketing and advertising?

Kate and her teachers celebrating Talk Like a Pirate Day, September 19

You may be celebrating the more traditional holidays, but the calendar is chock full of what I call "oddball holidays". Such as "Talk Like a Pirate Day" on September 19, or "Children's Book Week" in mid-May. Of course, there's the Week of the Young Child in April, and don't forget "National Chocolate Chip Day" on May 15. You can easily incorporate oddball holidays in your social media posts, on your signage, in your Parent Newsletter, and best of all, as a "reason why" you are launching a specific enrollment promotion.

For example, you could celebrate National Literacy Month in August by mailing inexpensive children's books to the homes of your clients and prospects (or purchase a list of households with children in your best neighborhoods). In the letter that accompanies the book, be sure to highlight the holiday in the headline, letting the recipient know why you're sending the book and what special offer they'll get when they enroll during the month of August. This is just one way to use an important "oddball" holiday to demonstrate how important reading and learning is to your customers and prospects, which will make them more likely to want to do business with you (or spread positive word of mouth about you to their neighbors and colleagues).

So get out your calendar and start planning which holidays you're going to tie your marketing into this year, and get your team to help with the creative brainstorming.

Priorities and Mindset

Idea #74:

Make Time to Market

So many times I find that owners and directors are not spending enough time on their marketing and enrollment-building. How much time is enough?

Well, first and foremost I believe you should "always be marketing". Even if your program is full, you need to market so you can keep your pipeline full with prospects. When you get complacent, you'll find that you took your eye off the ball and all of a sudden you're in trouble.

> **RESOURCE**
>
> To help you manage priorities and rid your life of "time vampires" I created a course called The Ultimate Time Management Guide for Child Care Leaders. Learn more here:
> **www.childcare-marketing. com/time**

As a guideline, if you are less than 60% full, you need to make marketing and customer satisfaction a massive priority in your business. I recommend spending at least one full day per week (or 8 to 10 hours split out into chunks) on marketing.

If you are 60-80% full, you should be spending 4 to 6 hours per week on marketing. And this includes the phone call and tour effectiveness. It makes no sense to spend time and money getting your phone to ring, if you're not converting those leads to enrollments.

If you are more than 80% full, congratulations – you are in the "sweet spot". Nearly every enrollment you get from 80 to 100% is pure profit because your expenses are covered. Spend 2 to 4 hours per week on marketing and customer retention activities.

Idea #75:
Implement to Completion

You've heard of the "bright shiny object syndrome", right? Some of us are more susceptible to this than others. However, we all fall victim at one time or another of being taken off task by some new glitzy idea sure to bring in more revenue or save costs.

You may eventually get back to the original project you were working on, but in the meantime, in those days, weeks, or months, how much money did you leave on the table?

You simply must learn to be more disciplined about implementing each idea or strategy TO COMPLETION. The ideas in this book will do you no good if you get each of them 50 to 70% complete. All you'll have is a handful of incomplete projects and no revenue or growth to show for all your effort.

If you must, hire someone whose job it is to track all ongoing projects in the company and keep the project "champions" on track and accountable to meet the deadlines they originally set. This is often referred to as a project manager. Even better - ask your directors to be project managers for areas they are passionate about, and split the duties.

Idea #76
Don't Follow the Crowd in Your Market

If you only take away one success secret from this book, let it be this one. This alone could explode your income and give you a HUGE advantage over your competition! This concept is not new. Earl Nightingale, considered to be the father of Personal Development, described this in his program Lead the Field. It goes like this:

"If you want to achieve success in any endeavor, and have not an example to follow, look at what everyone else is doing and do the opposite. Because the majority is always wrong." – Earl Nightingale

This can be said for pretty much anything in life, but it can be HUGE when it comes to your marketing.

Throughout this book, you may have come across a lot of uncommon marketing strategies that might make you feel a little "uneasy" or you'll question whether or not they'll work for you. That's because what you're learning in this book is vastly different then what the *majority* teaches about marketing and advertising—and probably what you've heard as well.

You're here because what you've been doing to market your child care business hasn't been working. Or your business has stagnated and you're looking for more "arrows in your quiver" you can pull out and summon more customers and clients at the drop of a hat.

And to accomplish this, you simply need to do what most of your competitors will not! You simply need to "go against the grain" of how other people in your industry market themselves—or "how things are done around here" in your market.

So the question for you is this: what are you going to do differently? You've already been presented with a whole host of marketing strategies in this book your competitors will NEVER know, or take action on. You just have to take massive action and implement them into your own business—and the success and prosperity you desire will be inevitable.

Idea #77:
Believe Things Can Be Different

So many times I've worked with owners and directors who are a victim of their own negative mindsets. This is what I and other coaches refer to as "stinkin' thinkin'." If you are trapped by your own negative thoughts, you are likely making excuses for why things aren't getting done, why your market or customers are different, why your staff never does what you tell them, why the parents you serve don't appreciate you, and so on and so on.

So how can you break free from these negative ways of thinking?

- Surround yourself with positive influences. Of course, this also means eliminating negative influences from your life – negative media, naysayers, and "why me" people all must go!

- Get help from mentors and coaches.

- Network with others who are where you want to be.

- Examine your beliefs and fears. See if you can identify their source and challenge their validity.

- Write down your goals and post them where you can see them.

- Visualize your "ideal day" and write out specifically what takes place in that day. Work towards making your ideal life a reality. This alone will empower you to make positive changes.

- Believe! Use the many case studies in this book to demonstrate that there are many owners and directors in our field who have achieved amazing results just by taking baby steps to bigger action.

You can do this. Now get started.

Bonus Idea #78:
Satisfaction Guarantee

In today's complex and skeptical world, trust trumps all when it comes to important purchase decisions. The child care decision is perhaps the most trust-based decision a parent can make. You need to add as many elements to your program as you can that demonstrate trust and peace of mind to parents.

That's why a satisfaction guarantee works so well for those of my clients brave enough to use one. I say "brave" because many leaders are fearful that parents will take advantage of them if they offer a guarantee. Ninety-nine percent of the time this simply does not happen, so once clients try it and see how much it benefits their enrollment, they continue to offer it.

I recommend naming your guarantee something fun that fits under the early childhood umbrella, such as the "Happy Family Guarantee" or "100 Percent Smiles Guarantee". The terms of the guarantee might look something like this:

The XYZ Happy Family Guarantee

We are so sure that you will love your experience with us that if at any time during your first 30 days of enrollment you wish to leave, we'll refund your money...no questions asked!

Put your guarantee on your website, your brochure, and in other marketing materials. It will grab the attention of parents because a satisfaction guarantee in child care is relatively rare (I'm sure your competitors don't have one) and it says "we believe in our service and our excellence". If you aren't ready to stand behind your service 100 percent, that's a signal that you may need to lead your team to a new level and vision of quality and excellence in your organization.

Conclusion

It is my sincere wish that you take a couple of these ideas and apply them as soon as possible to your marketing and enrollment-building plan. Hundreds (if not thousands) of early childhood business owners have used these strategies to massively grow their schools. Now it's your turn.

There are probably hundreds of reasons you could procrastinate, delay, and put off taking action – but I hope you won't fall into that common trap that all business owners and leaders face.

So get started today working "on" your business rather than just "in" it. Make an action plan, set deadlines, block time in your calendar, gather the troops to help you, and march forth.

Please send me an email with your results and success stories – it's what keeps me going! You can reach me directly at:

kris@childcare-marketing.com

All the best to you, your staff, the families you serve, and your community at large.

~ Kris

The Most Amazing Free Gift Ever

$554.94 of Pure Enrollment Growing Information –
YOURS FREE

Here's the scoop...when you sign up for the
Amazing Free Gift package, you will receive:

 FREE GIFT #1: *Staff Training DVD "How to Put On Your Sales Hat in Early Childhood Without Appearing Sales-Y".* A great tool for transforming your staff into your marketing partners. In this DVD, you will get actionable ideas for turning your staff meeting into a strategic session for gaining "buy-in" and partnership from your teachers and directors, in regards to growing your enrollment. This is an invaluable tool for engaging your team and transforming them into your enrollment-building partners. *Retail value: $97.00*

 FREE GIFT #2: *Audio CD "The #1 Thing You Can Do To Immediately Get More Enrollments for Your Child Care Program".* *Retail value: $67.00*

 FREE GIFT #3: *Audio CD "The #1 Secret to Becoming a Highly Successful & Profitable Child Care Business Owner".* *Retail value: $67.00*

 FREE GIFT #4: *Step-by-Step Workbook "Easy Steps for Measuring the Success of Your Marketing & Enrollment-Building Efforts".* Most business owners, including child care owners, simply don't keep score of their core business "metrics". This guide will take you through the 9 essential metrics you need to track in your child care program, if you want to easily and quickly grow your enrollment and get to full capacity. *Retail value: $127.00.*

FREE GIFT #5: *Special Top-Secret Audio Interview with Ms. X "How I Opened My Brand New Early Childhood Center With a Waiting List of 48 Children".* Listen in as I interview "Ms. X" a child care start-up with little to no early education experience. Ms. X opened her new preschool 100% full with a waiting list of 48 children, in an inner-city neighborhood. Use the strategies Ms. X reveals to get fully enrolled quickly, or open up your new location in a highly successful manner. *Retail value: $97.00*

 FREE GIFT #6: *Two Months FREE TRIAL of Kris Murray's Insiders Circle* featuring monthly newsletters, audio CDs with experts each month, actual examples of real marketing pieces, ads, flyers, etc. that you can "model", what's working for other programs around the country, and much more! *Retail value: $99.94.*

www.ChildCare-Marketing.com/AmazingFreeGift